Land Navigation Handbook

Sierra Club Outdoor Adventure Guides

Simple Foods for the Pack
More than 200 all-natural, trail-tested recipes
by Claudia Axcell, Vikki Kinmont Kath, and Diana Cooke

Walking Softly in the Wilderness
The Sierra Club Guide to Backpacking
by John Hart

Land Navigation Handbook

The Sierra Club Guide to Map, Compass & GPS

Second Edition

W. S. Kals

Completely updated, with new text by Clyde Soles

Sierra Club Books

San Francisco

Copyright © 2005 by Clyde Soles
Copyright © 1983 by Ann C. Ten Eyck

Published by Sierra Club Books
85 Second Street, San Francisco, CA 94105
www.sierraclub.org/books

Produced and distributed by
University of California Press
Berkeley and Los Angeles, California
University of California Press, Ltd.
London, England
www.ucpress.edu

Library of Congress Cataloging-in-Publication Data

Kals, W. S.

   Land navigation handbook : the Sierra Club guide to map, compass & GPS /
     by W. S. Kals. — 2nd ed. / completely updated, with new text by Clyde Soles.
       p. cm. — (A Sierra Club outdoor adventure guide)
     Includes index.
     ISBN 1-57805-122-3 (alk. paper)   ISBN 13 978-1-57805-122-9
      1. Orienteering—Handbooks, manuals, etc. 2. Maps—Handbooks,
     manuals, etc. 3. Navigation—Handbooks, manuals, etc. I. Soles, Clyde,
     1959– II. Sierra Club. III. Title. IV. Series.
   GV200.4.K34 2005
   796.58—dc22   2004065085

Book and cover design by Lynne O'Neil
Composition by David Van Ness
Cover photo © Scott Atkinson
Interior photos © Clyde Soles
Maps on pages 46, 93, 120, 121, 123, 124, and 161 by William Nelson

Printed in the United States of America on New Leaf Ecobook 50 acid-free paper, which contains a minimum of 50 percent post-consumer waste, processed chlorine free. Of the balance, 25 percent is Forest Stewardship Council certified to contain no old-growth trees and to be pulped totally chlorine free.

Second Edition

09 08 07 06

10 9 8 7 6 5 4 3 2

Contents

Preface to the Second Edition

It has been a privilege to revise what is certainly a classic instructional text for the outdoors. *Land Navigation Handbook* has been in print for over twenty years and has educated countless readers on map and compass skills.

Although the basics of navigation haven't changed since W. S. Kals first penned this title, the technology sure has. I bought my first personal computer in 1983, the same year the first edition of this book was published. That computer came with 16 kilobytes of RAM, used a cassette tape player for data storage, and could print only crude black text—using that system for navigation was unfathomable.

In that same year, the Global Positioning System (a by-product of the Cold War) was first made available to the public. But using GPS technology required massive receivers that were not exactly portable. It wasn't until about 1993 that the first handheld GPS units became available, and those were big, expensive, and primitive by today's standards.

Now, of course, powerful home computers may have a gigabyte of RAM (over 65,000 times more than my 1983 computer held) and huge hard drives, while photo-quality color printers are commonplace. Some of the current GPS receivers can be worn on your wrist, are cheaper than many cameras, and a few can even display topographic maps on the screen.

With these technological advances, navigation has become much easier. But often the manuals leave users more confused than ever, and they never explain the basic skills still required. Marketing departments may try to convince you that map and compass knowledge are no longer necessary—nothing could be further from the truth.

One of the great strengths of Kals's writing is his ability to explain complicated concepts in simple terms. I've tried to complement, rather than intrude upon, his material while bringing it up to date. This new edition should be useful for many years to come.

— Clyde Soles
February 2005

Preface to the Second Edition

1.

Land Navigation

Some of us learned to navigate the way a foal learns horse business: by trotting alongside mother. At other times we may have learned the kangaroo way, by being carried along. Still later, we likely navigated by watching the heels of the person in front of us.

Many hikers never advance beyond the latter technique. They simply follow other people, guidebook descriptions, and trail signs without ever learning basic navigation skills.

One difficulty in only following markers and trails is that you never know how long it'll take you to reach your destination. If you are lucky enough to find a sign at the trailhead giving a time estimate, double it to be on the safe side, at least until you establish a more accurate factor. If the sign gives a distance rather than a time, count on making no more than 1 to 1½ miles (1½ to 2½ kilometers) per hour. If you carry cameras, children, or both, you won't even make that.

But you'll get there eventually—in good summer weather.

Fog may not let you see the next marker or sign. Snow wipes out all signs of a footway surprisingly quickly. Wind-driven snow obliterates blazes, paint, and other markers. If you try to retrace your steps— as you should—you'll find that the landscape looks completely unfamiliar. Unless, of course, you turned around often on the way in and memorized what the world looks like when you walk the other way.

You should do that even if you do not intend to return by the same trail. Weather, a washed-out foot-bridge, or some minor mishap may force you to execute that popular and highly recommended course change: a 180° turn.

Following marked trails is not advanced navigation, but it beats heel watching.

It won't be long before you'll want a map—a map that lets you determine your own routes and how long they should take at your pace. Often, a map alone can tell you where you are, without the need for a compass.

This may make it sound as if a map could solve most problems of navigation. Within some limits, it can.

For instance, you could walk the Appalachian Trail from Springer Mountain, Georgia, to Mount Katahdin, Maine, without a map. But how would you find the post office where your next supply of freeze-dried food and mail is waiting? Without a map, how would you even know where to mail your supplies?

Chapter 2 may tell you more about maps than you wish to know. But this book is not only for people whose hiking strategy is to follow others. It should also serve as a refresher for those who are a bit rusty in land navigation. Even experts will find new information in this book, and those experienced in small-craft navigation will learn to apply what they already know in new ways.

Because sea kayaking is usually performed within sight of land, some basic information on nautical charts and currents is included. Most near shore navigation techniques are related to the landscape.

You will learn how to decode map symbols and to read distance, height, and direction from a map. With practice, you can answer such questions as, How steep is the trail? How long will it take me if I'm traveling uphill, or downhill? With new computer mapping software, these questions become even easier to answer.

Once you're familiar with topographic maps and nautical charts, the whole world becomes your playground. You'll be able to sight-read maps in Canada, the Andes, the Himalayas, or the Austrian Alps. The differences in details are small and are usually stated on the maps themselves.

The Austrian map, for example, will show symbols used to distinguish between a cable car, a chair lift, a ski tow, and a freight lift that may or may not carry your pack to the hut. The fact that it uses meters and kilometers rather than feet and miles will hardly bother you.

By the time you have reached the subject of reading directions from the map—if not earlier—you'll want a compass.

There are certain situations in which you can navigate using a compass without a map. But land navigation, like basic marine navigation, is mainly map-and-compass work. And map and compass are the only tools you'll need, although you may find a dime-store ruler useful, and sometimes a pencil stub.

Binoculars, although not counted as navigational tools by most writers, are as helpful in spotting and identifying the next marker as they are in marine navigation. A compact pair of binoculars is smaller than a deck of cards, weighs only 5 ounces, and can enhance any trip.

A compass helps you solve navigational problems such as, If I'm here—say on the peak of a mountain— what mountain is that over there? Or, often more useful, Over there is Mount Onthemap, so where on the Appalachian Trail am I?

You'll read about *position lines,* a concept that ties together these and other navigational problems. Advanced marine navigators may call them *lines of position*—LOPs for short.

With an altimeter to measure your elevation, you'll learn to fix your position on the map even when bad weather prevents you from seeing past the tips of your skis.

The Global Positioning System (GPS) is without a doubt a marvelous aid for navigation. A handheld receiver can help you pinpoint your location almost anywhere on the planet to within a few feet. However, to be a competent outdoorsperson, you must first learn basic map and compass skills.

No book on land navigation is complete without instructions for finding directions from the sky. You'll also read about methods that work in the tropics and in the Southern Hemisphere, where the polestar can't be seen.

In Chapter 13, you'll find some useful concepts and tips. Many of them derive from orienteering, a competitive sport that combines running with map and compass work. Devised at the end of the nineteenth century by military messengers in Scandinavia, orienteering has become popular in the United States, Canada, Great Britain, and some sixty other countries. Many adventure races have orienteering segments to challenge competitors mentally as well as physically.

Orienteering competitions are usually staged in hilly woods, but the tips given in Chapter 13 are useful outside of competitions and in any terrain. These are the techniques that separate the casual hiker whose comfort zone is on trails from the veteran navigator who can find the most efficient way over an unfamiliar landscape.

Perhaps the most important navigation technique of all is common sense. There will be times when the unexpected happens. Don't just charge ahead with grit and determination; often, this only makes the situation worse. Stop and consider all the possibilities before making your plan of action.

2.

Maps & Map Symbols

The challenge for mapmakers is to create a depiction of a landscape that viewers can use to correctly interpret what is around them and what is out of sight. This representation is typically rendered on a flat surface, be it paper or a screen, so a sense of vertical dimension needs to be included.

The viewpoint of the representation should also be mentioned in the definition. You have probably seen paintings of mountains with chairlifts and hiking trails or ski runs shown in perspective. The artist seems to have stood on a mountain—real or imagined—looking north or south or whatever. Maps always show the land seen from directly above.

Of course, they also show it greatly reduced in size. A map the size of Rocky Mountain National Park—about 21 by 26 miles (34 by 42 kilometers)—would be awkward to handle. A sheet roughly 28 by 38 inches (71 by 97 centimeters) is handier.

To be really useful, directions on maps should be related to directions in nature. Trails that cross at right angles should be shown crossing at the same angles on the map. And it should be possible to read geographic directions from a map. By custom, geographic North on maps is at the top. A point that in nature is directly North of another one will be directly above it on the map.

Also, distances on maps should be related to distances in nature. Points 2 miles apart should be shown twice as far apart on the map as points only 1 mile apart.

Cartography

Although many maps were derived from aerial photographs, most are not photographs themselves but drawings based on photographs with graphic symbols—say a tent for a campsite—added. The overlapping aerial photographs of mapmakers are supplemented by ground surveys that locate control points within the area to be mapped and measure the precise elevation of many points. Some points may serve as both horizontal and vertical controls.

Here's how maps were made from aerial photographs. The photograph was projected onto a sheet of plastic on which the control points were accurately plotted. The size of the projected image was then adjusted, and the drawing shifted until two photographed control points fell exactly on the marks on the paper, just as a photographer adjusts his enlarger for size and moves the paper holder to get the image where he wants it.

Only rarely will the other control points project right onto their marks on the drawing. Why? Everyone who has ever taken a photograph of a tall building can answer that: tilting the camera to get the top of the building into the picture makes the building in the photograph narrower at the top than at the bottom. Perhaps the plane's nose was up, tilting the camera and making the distance between marks ahead less than it should have been.

Unlike simple photographic enlargers, the projectors used in mapmaking let you tilt the negative (and the table) to correct for that. On the first try the marks will probably be closer to the drawn ones, but not quite in place yet. Perhaps one wing of the plane was somewhat higher than the other at the time of the exposure.

If the plane was flying north, a tilt in the east-west direction of negative and table will correct that.

Buildings, roads, railroads, and other artificial features, all of which will be printed in black, were then scribed onto the plastic sheet. Since 1998, this has changed to digital production methods.

Later, place-names were added. For example, a radio tower is marked, like other landmarks, as a dot in the center of a small circle. It's certainly a fine landmark, but of little use without the legend that tells you it is not a chimney, a water tower, or a historical monument.

Place-names may have come from older maps, but much additional information had to be gathered by field investigation.

Creeks, banks of rivers, and other waterways as well as lakes and ponds go on a printing plate that will be inked blue.

On the plate to be inked red are drawn section and township lines, fences and edges of fields, and the fill on highways.

On the plate to be inked green are drawn the areas covered with woods, orchards, scattered trees, and shrubs.

Information is added in the margins of the map, such as the identification of the area, and everything is checked. Then the map is printed in each of the colors, in exact register with the first one printed, on the same sheet. Trimming the margins finishes the map.

Topographic Maps

For many readers—hikers, backpackers, fishermen, hunters, skiers—and for those planning highways, pipelines, and so on, such a map is not good enough. What they need is a *topographic* map.

It does not help a bit to know that the word comes from the Greek words *topos,* "a place," and *graphein,* "to write or draw." All maps describe or draw places. Topographic maps clearly show the topography, the ups and downs of the landscape, as opposed to *plani-metric* maps, which show the land as though it were all at one level.

The map whose development from aerial photographs you just read about is a planimetric map. So are political maps in an atlas, which might show the United States in green, Canada in pink, Mexico in purple, and so on.

Other maps in the same atlas—physical maps—use colors to show elevations above sea level. Everything between sea level and 500 feet may be bluish green; above that but below 1,000 feet, a lighter shade of the same tint; 1,000 to 2,000 feet, beige; 2,000 to 5,000 feet, a lighter beige; 5,000 to 10,000 feet, yellow; and everything above that, white.

To make a planimetric map into a topographic map requires one more color—brown, for example—to be printed in perfect register with the other colors.

The process that translates aerial photographs into squiggles for the brown printing plate is based on the stereoscope, a century-old viewing gadget. Looking through that device at photographs taken with two cameras (or one camera with two lenses side by side), Victorians could see Albert Hall, the Taj Mahal, the Matterhorn, or the fat lady from the circus in three dimensions.

A popular early application of stereoscopic vision was 3-D movies. Two cameras were used to shoot the picture; the film taken with one was projected in red, the other in blue. The patrons were given spectacles with a red filter for one eye and a blue one for the other. Wearing these specs they could thrill to a stomach-knotting roller-coaster ride or watch a pair of lions eat their way through a sleeping car full of people, all seemingly in three dimensions.

In the production of topographic maps, two aerial photographs taken miles apart were projected through red and blue filters. The operator of the sophisticated stereoplotter looked through red and blue glasses.

He first adjusted both images for tilt of the plane fore and aft and wing to wing at the time the pictures were taken. Then he looked for one of the vertical control points. He raised or lowered the table onto which the images were projected until the two images of the control point fused into one.

By the laws of optics, all points at the same elevation, and only these points, fuse. The operator then traced a line connecting all these points. That line became the contour line at the elevation of the vertical control point. He then raised the table a predetermined distance and traced the next contour. You'll read about these contours in more detail in Chapter 4, "Height from the Map." For now you may just want to look at the foldout map inside the back cover of this book and glance at the wiggly brown lines. That should give you a better feel for what makes a topographic map than any dictionary definition.

Topographic maps (topo maps) in this country are very accurate; from start to finish, it took about five years to produce a single map using traditional methods. Here are the standards of accuracy for United States Geological Survey (USGS) topo maps on the scale of the foldout map in the back of this book, the very popular 7.5-minute (7½′) series in which 1 inch on the map corresponds to 2,000 feet in the field.

Horizontally. No more than 10 percent of well-defined test points may be more than ¹⁄₅₀ inch (about ½ millimeter) from their true position. On 1:24,000-scale maps, this means about 40 feet (12 meters).

Vertically. No more than 10 percent of the test point elevations may be more than one-half contour interval off. The contour interval—the difference from one printed contour to the next—on the foldout map, as on many of these maps in mountainous regions, is 40 feet; 90 percent of all points checked on these maps must be within 20 feet (6 meters) of their true height above sea level. In flat country, where the contour interval typically is 10 feet, they'd have to be within 5 feet (1½ meters).

That's certainly accurate enough for hiking, skiing, hunting, fishing. And it's good enough to plan a road, a real estate development, a ski lift, or a pipeline.

Do topographic maps, such as the foldout map inside the back cover, tell the whole truth? No, and you would not want them to. You wouldn't want them cluttered with every chicken coop, woodshed, and outhouse. They show that an area is not wooded, but is it bare rock or meadow? The map does not say.

And all maps show things that you won't see in the landscape. Have you ever seen a meridian of longitude, or a parallel of latitude? Or the lines that enclose a section of land, or form borders of counties or national forests?

Also, time makes liars out of maps. By the time they are printed they are already partially out of date as changes subsequently occur. An area is not wooded anymore, a road has been straightened, a railroad track has been torn up. New houses have been built, a new dam has created a lake, a mangrove swamp has been filled and seeded with townhouses.

In 1992, the USGS finished mapping all of the lower forty-eight states and Hawaii for the 7½′ primary series—over 54,000 maps! Alaska still relies on smaller scale (1:63,360) maps, except around Anchorage, Fairbanks, and Prudhoe Bay, where large-scale maps are available. With that half-century-long project complete, the focus now is on digitizing and revising the maps.

The easiest way to revise maps to show changes in areas was to overprint existing maps. The corrections were printed in purple. Now, maps are revised using computerized raster (bitmap) image and vector graphic files. Due to the expense and time required, and a shift in funding priorities, revised maps are seldom field-checked against "ground truth."

The USGS is currently digitizing all of the topographic maps by scanning each separate layer used to build them. Thus, instead of the single scan that consumer mapping software produces, this process yields about ten levels of detail, such as contours, roads, streams, wooded areas, buildings, and so forth. While it is of particular value to business and government, the raster revision mapping project will ultimately result in more accurate maps for the rest of us.

Map Margins

To make the best use of the space, our foldout map has no margins. Likewise, some weight-conscious backpackers are rumored to cut off the margins of their maps.

But margins are full of useful information, some of which is discussed more fully in Chapters 3, 4, and 5. Other information found in map margins is of little importance for walking, skiing, or canoeing, but you may want to know what it is all about.

What follows comes from the margins that have been cut from our foldout map (see Figure 2.1).

In the top right corner you'll find the map title:

FALL RIVER PASS QUADRANGLE,
COLORADO
7.5 Minute Series (Topographic)

The map title uniquely describes this map. The name of the state is important, since some quadrangle names may be duplicated elsewhere. With more than 2,000 maps covering Colorado alone, it would be difficult for the vendor to mail you the right map without knowing the state in which the quadrangle lies.

All quads of the lower forty-eight states and Hawaii are named for some prominent feature on that sheet, such as a peak, a lake, or a town.

The "7.5 Minute" part of the title becomes clear when you look at the bottom right corner of the map. It's marked 40°22′30″ for north latitude, while the top right corner is labeled 40°30′. The difference is 7′30″, or 7½′. The bottom right and top corners are marked 105°45′ for west longitude, and the left corners read 105°52′30″. The difference is again 7½′. All maps of this series cover 7½′ latitude and 7½′ longitude.

The title is repeated in slightly altered form in the bottom right corner:

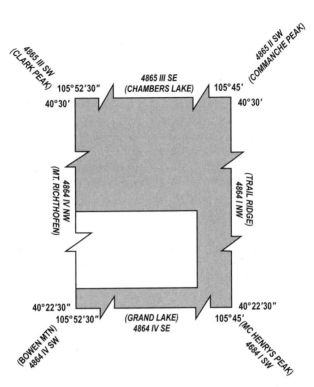

Figure 2.1 Latitude, longitude, and titles of adjoining maps shown in the margins of the Fall River Pass quad. White area shows the coverage of the foldout map in the back of this book.

FALL RIVER PASS, COLO
N4022.5-W10545 / 7.5

You'll recognize the abbreviated latitude—latitude by custom is always given first—and longitude from the bottom right corner of the map itself. (If you have trouble remembering the difference between latitude and longitude, try this old saying: "A tropical latitude improves my attitude.") The bottom right corner is a logical place to start the count of the 7.5′ since latitude in this part of the world increases upward, longitude toward the left. Both directions are easily memorized— they are exactly opposite to the way we write.

However, this system of designating the maps has been replaced. If Fall River Pass ever sees another revision, it will be labeled 40105-D7-TF-024. The "40105" gives the map's position in degrees. The "D7" places the map relative to a group of sixty-four maps (an eight-by-eight grid). "TF" means that it's a topographic map measured in feet. And "024" tells us that the map is in 1:24,000 scale.

Using this grid system, the map to the right (Trail Ridge, Colo.) is designated D6 and the map to the left (Mount Richthofen, Colo.) is D8. The map directly below Fall River Pass (Grand Lake, Colo.) is C7 and the map above (Chambers Lake, Colo.) is E7.

In the top left corner of the margin you'll find this credit line:

United States
Department of the Interior
Geological Survey

The explanation is in the bottom left corner in a notice similar to this:

Mapped, edited and published by the Geological Survey as part of the Department of the Interior program for the development of the Missouri River Basin

Underneath that you often find another statement: "Control by USGS [that's our friends, the Geological Survey] and NOS/NOAA [National Ocean Service/ National Oceanic and Atmospheric Administration]," meaning that both agencies provided vertical and horizontal ground controls.

Modern maps also carry the statement "Topography from aerial photographs by photogrammetric methods." That refers to the stereo method described earlier. Our map's aerial photographs were taken in 1953 and field-checked in 1958. The map remained unchanged until 1977 and is unlikely to be revised again for many years to come.

That's not as bad as it sounds. The important topography will not have changed. Roads may have either improved or deteriorated. New trails may have been built, some may have been realigned to protect sensitive areas, and still others may have disappeared for lack of upkeep.

National park and national forest offices are a good source of information on trails. They issue maps not nearly as useful for topography as the 7½' quads but that show every trail and fire road in the area. By all means, get one. The map will show numbers for the footways and jeep trails. The numbers are likely to be posted at each trailhead, which makes land navigation easier.

A purple notice in the margin of our 7½' map shows that it was revised from aerial photographs taken in 1976 that were not field-checked.

The legend at the bottom of the map continues, "Polyconic projection, 1927 North American datum." The first part describes the method by which the approximately spherical earth has been translated onto the flat sheet of the map. The datum is the surveyor's initial point used as the basic reference point for maps of the United States, Canada, Mexico, and Central American countries. (It is located on the Meades Ranch in central Kansas, west and a little south of Waldo, which you may find on a map on Route 281, north of I-70. The datum coordinates are N39°13'26.686" and W098°32'30.506".)

Then come some notes that tie the specific map into a larger system of maps. On our map they read, "10,000-foot grid based on Colorado coordinate system, north zone. 1,000-meter Universal Transverse Mercator grid ticks, zone 13, shown in blue."

Some maps also provide information on how to offset the map so that it agrees with the newer 1983 North American (1984 World Geodetic System) Datum used by satellites. The lower left and upper right corners of the map will sometimes have a dashed cross that shows the difference between the two datums; in some places the datums can be offset by more than 600 feet. This is only important if you forget to change the datum on your GPS unit. Another line states that this map complies with National Map Accuracy Standards. That's the accuracy standard you read about earlier.

Some maps, including ours, show a key to road classification.

Ah, yes, and then there is a commercial: "For sale by U.S. Geological Survey, Denver, Colorado 80225, or Reston, Virginia 22092."

And a free bonus: "A folder describing topographic maps and symbols is available on request."

Map Symbols

The master key to colors on topographic maps, reduced to its simplest applications, specifies green for woodlands, brown for contours, blue for water, red for roads and survey lines, and black for artificial objects, including names. These categories all appear on our map.

However, it is unlikely that a single map will show all possible map symbols. For example, you are not likely to find tropical mangroves, a glacier, and an urban area together.

Symbols Printed in Black

Some of the symbols printed in black ink are straightforward and don't require interpretation. If you saw the mast of a ship and part of its hull jutting at an odd angle from a blue area, you'd assume it symbolizes a wreck.

Other symbols are labeled or can be interpreted easily. For example, broken black lines mark boundaries. Different line weights and dash lengths are used for national, state, county, and other boundaries. One boundary runs across our map: the Continental Divide. No question there. Elsewhere, you might find a broken line with the label "Colorado" on one side and "Utah" on the other. Again, no need to memorize the line code.

You may already know that little black squares or T- or L-shapes indicate buildings. (On maps made prior to 1991, black shading indicates unoccupied buildings.) The only two buildings on our map strad-dle the red squares numbered 7 and 12.

A black square with a pennant indicates a school; with a cross, it means a church. A cross inside a dashed enclosure indicates a cemetery. For large cemeteries, you'll find the letters "Cem" inside the enclosure.

There are no railroads on our map. But if you saw a black line with cross ties, you'd figure out its meaning.

Telephone lines, pipelines, and so on—black dashed lines—are always labeled. Power lines are dashed lines with large dots symbolizing the supports; metal towers are shown as tiny squares at the exact location.

For many readers, the most interesting black lines are the dashed trail lines. Several labeled trails are on our map, for example, the Red Mountain Trail near the bottom left corner.

It starts near the two houses at the end of two par-allel lines that indicate a rather poor road. According to the key printed on the map itself (but cut off in our sample), it's a light-duty road with a hard or improved surface. Had the road been unimproved, say a fire access road, it would be shown by two interrupted lines, like a string of equal signs.

An X-mark or triangle with a dot in the center, with or without the abbreviation *BM* or *VABM*, gives the exact point where the elevation printed next to it has been measured. These are discussed in Chapter 4.

The symbols shown in Figure 2.2 are the ones you are likely to encounter printed in black.

And don't forget the landmark symbol—a circle with a dot in the center. The dot gives the exact location of almost anything. Some of the labels used are more obvious than others (e.g., Lookout or Campsite). A few useful examples: TR for tower, hence R TR for radio tower, TV TR for television tower; MON for monument.

In addition, if you look carefully, you will notice four crosses in the same location on each topographic map. These are the intersections of meridians and par-allels of latitude that divide the map area into thirds (not including the margins, so they are not fold

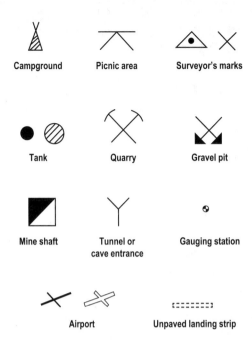

Figure 2.2 Map symbols that are always printed in black. For colored symbols, see the foldout map in the back of this book.

marks). On the map from which ours was cut, you'll see one cross near the middle, near Squeak Creek, and another just below Peak 11,961.

Along the edge of each map, you will find black tick marks and a number (often very large) in feet. These refer to a state grid system used for describing parcels of land. For our purposes, you can ignore them.

Symbols Printed in Color

Red is used for hard-surface roads; solid is used for primary highways interrupted—as on our map—for secondary highways. If you saw a fat red line with a black line through the center, you would probably figure out that it's a divided highway. When the dividing strip is more than 25 feet (8 meters) wide, the two red lines are separated.

Red is also used for survey lines, like the rectangles and squares on our map, and for fence and field lines. A red tint (see the bottommost symbol alongside our map) was used to show a built-up area where streets and buildings are omitted; newer maps use gray.

All water features are printed in blue. So are permanent snowfields and glaciers. The tick marks for the Universal Transverse Mercator (UTM) grid system are also printed in blue just outside the perimeter of the map.

Our map shows many ponds, and several lakes and streams. All of the streams are less than 25 feet wide and hence are shown as single blue lines.

That includes the mighty Colorado River, which runs south past the two buildings on our map. If the river were more than 25 feet wide, the map would show its banks with blue between. But here the Colorado River is close to its source and thus very small. Less than a mile north of the top of our map, the trail, which started out as the Colorado River Trail and became the La Poudre Pass Trail, crosses the Colorado. Even with a fully loaded backpack you can jump across it.

The Grand Ditch, near the left margin of our map, is also less than 25 feet wide. The word *grand* refers not to size or the marvel of it but to the earlier name of the Colorado, Grand River, which was officially changed in 1921.

The Grand Ditch, with its parallel service road, was built in the 1890s, mostly with pick and shovel by Asian laborers. Its purpose: to bring one-third of the rainfall and snowmelt from the west slope of the Never Summer Mountains to the arid eastern side of the Continental Divide—the first theft of water from the Pacific side by the Atlantic side. Half the water goes to the city of Thornton and the remainder goes to farmers in northeastern Colorado.

Acclaimed in its day, the Grand Ditch was added to the National Register of Historic Places in 1976. A major breach in 2003 that scarred the land and several earlier breaches have put the future of this water diversion project in question.

You won't have much trouble reading or remembering the other map symbols printed in blue.

One warning: when you are canoeing or kayaking, don't trust the rapids and falls symbols on the map. They are easily overlooked, the mapmaker's small falls may turn out to be Class 5 rapids, and a thrilling ride at one water level can become a death trap at another. Get local information from someone with current knowledge.

You'll read a lot more about contour lines, printed in brown, in Chapter 4.

The symbols for a road cut and road fill are tricky. Look closely; you'll be able to read them only if you recognize depression contours—contours with little barbs pointing downhill.

The best way to familiarize yourself with maps and map symbols is to use them. One way is to obtain a topo map of your neighborhood or some area you know well and take mental walks, recognizing on the map many of the familiar landmarks. Better yet, if possible, take a real walk with the map in hand.

The symbols used on U.S. topographic maps are also used on other U.S. maps, including those of lakes and rivers and the coastlines of nautical charts. Virtually the same symbols are used on maps of Canada and on official maps of the rest of the world.

If you hike abroad, say in the European Alps, you'll find some of the most useful maps are published not by government agencies but by private interests. The maps of the Austrian Alpine Club—available with or without ski routes—and the widely sold Kompass Wanderkarten series are good examples. They are based on government maps but have been redrawn to keep one group of mountains together on one sheet. Government maps split such areas along lines of latitude and longitude.

Both sets of maps mentioned above use red for trails rather than roads. (Roads are shown in yellow.) Different symbols are used for well-marked (and numbered) trails, less well-marked trails, and trails that in spots require technical skills. These and all other symbols not in the international code are decoded on the map itself. Kompass gives the legend in German, English, and French.

On the back of many Kompass maps you'll find suggested trips, lists of huts in the area, accommodations in the valley, and so on. You don't have to be fluent in German to get the drift.

Nautical Charts

Although this book's focus is *land* navigation, many readers may try sea kayaking someday. While USGS maps provide good detail of the land above the high-tide mark, they leave much to be desired out on the water. All coastal topos include bathymetric contours (provided by National Ocean Service), but these are of only limited value.

True nautical charts are updated about every two years and contain far more information that can help you plan trips and navigate the waters. We won't get into the minutiae, but a basic understanding of these maps is useful.

With nautical charts, you can identify distant buoys, channel markers, and lighthouses. You can "see" the shipping lanes and know where it's best to cross. You can predict where currents will be strong and where a tidal flat may leave you stranded far from the water.

As with land maps, charts come in different scales: small (1:80,000), medium (1:40,000), and large (1:20,000). The most useful are the medium-scale maps, also called general-scale maps, since they can cover an entire day's journey.

The official government maps are printed on one side of paper sheets. However, sea kayakers should purchase the commercial maps that are printed on both sides of waterproof paper (http://maptech.com and http://waterproofcharts.com). Note that these maps are resized, so scales vary.

Most charts sold today provide depths in meters. However, older charts in the United States often used feet and fathoms (1 fathom = 6 feet). This information is clearly marked in the title at the top center of the chart.

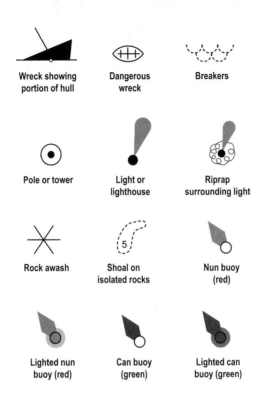

Wreck showing portion of hull

Dangerous wreck

Breakers

Pole or tower

Light or lighthouse

Riprap surrounding light

Rock awash

Shoal on isolated rocks

Nun buoy (red)

Lighted nun buoy (red)

Can buoy (green)

Lighted can buoy (green)

Figure 2.3 Nautical chart symbols.

Nautical charts contain minimal information about land—just enough for recognizing features. Land features are labeled with block letters; water features are printed in italics.

Once you are familiar with topographic maps, reading nautical charts is fairly straightforward. Sometimes there is more text than you are used to; for example, both horizontal and vertical clearance distances are given for bridges.

The symbols for buoy types can be confusing (see Figure 2.3), but the code printed next to each helps solve the mystery of what that blinking light is in the distance. If the chart reads FL G 4sec 10ft 4M "1", then you know that the buoy has a **FL**ashing **G**reen light, it flashes every **4 sec**onds, it is **10 feet** above the water, the buoy can be seen **4 miles** away, it has a big **1** painted on the sides, and it has a flat top.

Red buoys are always evenly numbered, have conical tops, and are kept on the starboard side when returning to land (Red Right Returning). Buoys that are both red and green mark the junctions of channels; use the topmost color for instructions on what to do.

If you will be sea kayaking on open water where tides are less of a factor, it may also be desirable to purchase a current chart such as *Reed's Nautical Almanac*. Since a sea kayak only averages about 2 to 3 knots, a 1-knot current can be either a huge boost or a hateful hindrance. With a current chart, you can plan to use or avoid currents and even to take advantage of eddies.

Digital Maps

Of all the electronic innovations from the past two decades, arguably the most useful for backcountry users is topo maps in digital format. Sure, a GPS unit can be handy. But, for the most part, you just don't need one.

Although the detail of our 7½′ (1:24,000) maps is wonderful, it can be a nuisance to go on a day hike that spans several topo maps, maybe just nipping the corner of one, and requires still others to identify nearby features.

With the new digital maps, you can select as much, or as little, terrain as you want, zoom in or out in scale, and print just that selection onto waterproof paper. The software allows "seamless" maps, where the borders are hidden, and lets you add your own trails and notes. These custom maps are easier to use and have features not possible with paper maps, such as shading, trail profiles, and sharing information with other users.

If you were to purchase 7½′ maps for just a quarter of the state of Colorado, the bill would come to roughly $3,000 and the stack of folded maps would be over 6 feet tall and weigh over 40 pounds. Yet you can purchase 1:24,000 digital maps for the entire state for

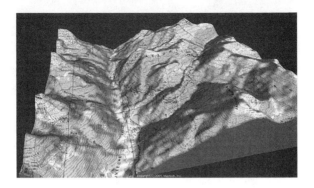

Figure 2.4 Digital 3-D rendering of the area covered in the foldout map; viewing height and direction are easily changed.

under $100 and they fit on eight compact discs (CDs). If you don't need that level of detail, a 1:100,000 topo of all fifty states costs only $50.

Users with GPS units can transfer information to and from the digital mapping software. This makes it very easy to input significant coordinates (e.g., trailheads, junctions, campsites) prior to the journey; from the trailhead, the GPS unit could lead you directly to your destination. It also allows you to easily record important locations in the field (e.g., a food cache, prime fishing hole, or scenic viewpoint) and add them to maps for future excursions.

All USGS maps are in the public domain, meaning our taxes paid for them. Thus, there are no copyright issues, so it is legal for companies to scan the maps and convert them to a digital format (better resolution) or use USGS digital raster graphics files.

What sets the various products apart are the value-added features such as updated trail information, route plotting, 3-D viewing, and aerial photo overlays. Many of these programs are now fourth-generation products, so the user interface is sophisticated but still friendly. Figure 2.4 is an example of a standard topo map rendered with the help of a computer.

Maps from most other governments are protected by copyrights, so these countries have been slower to offer digital maps for consumers, and they tend to be expensive. Currently, only Canada, Germany, Great Britain, New Zealand, and Switzerland have digital 1:50,000 topo maps readily available, though many more countries will be covered in the future.

If you have a flatbed scanner and a program such as OziExplorer, you can even create your own digital maps by scanning in almost any paper map. Once calibrated, these can be used like the commercial digital maps, though currently you cannot merge maps to create a larger seamless one.

Digital maps made from scans cannot be read directly by GPS units since they require vector maps. However, scanned maps can be merged with a GIS (geographic information system) file downloaded off the Internet (see, for instance, www.esri.com and www.gis.com) to create a map that can be uploaded to some GPS units.

It takes a reasonably powerful computer or a fast Internet connection (preferably both) to really enjoy the full benefits of digital topographic maps. A bit of geekiness helps too. Large, memory-intensive files can be painfully slow to work with on older machines, and you may not be able to access all their features. Until recently, Macintosh users faced the extra headache of using a Windows emulator, though, thankfully, native software is now slowly becoming available.

Printing Digital Maps

There are several options for making paper maps from digital files. The easiest is to print them at home using an inkjet printer; however, normal paper and ink won't hold up well. A cheap map that gets wet and disintegrates could turn your trip into an epic.

If you rely on maps printed at home, the best option is to use waterproof mapping paper made for inkjet printers. This is made from a single-layer, silica-based synthetic (not wood pulp) designed to absorb ink and offer high definition and excellent color rendition. Unless you have a more expensive printer that can handle wide paper, you are limited to letter (8.5 by 11 inches) or legal (8.5 by 14 inches) size. Although waterproof paper costs about $0.50 to $0.75 per sheet, you can print on both sides, the maps look great, and they are incredibly durable.

The more frugal will opt to use normal paper and then treat the maps afterward. If you go this route, select a very bright (92 or higher), fairly heavy (24 lb.) paper for best color rendition and reasonable durability; even this is too thin for two-sided printing. Cheap paper causes ink to spread, resulting in blurry details. Photo papers work but are usually coated on only one side and pricey—you might as well use mapping paper.

Inkjet printers that use a solvent base (ketone/alcohol) can print sharp images onto Tyvek, a rugged synthetic paper. However, water-based inks will feather and blur, which reduces image quality. With a Tyvek map laminated with clear plastic shelving paper on the front (lay the map face down onto the film, then use a roller to apply pressure), you get very flexible, nearly indestructible maps that you can make erasable notes on with an alcohol-based pen.

The really thrifty can print maps in black on a laser printer. For areas that are heavily forested, this actually works fairly well, since all the green doesn't add useful information and may hide some detail. But roads and streams can resemble contour lines, and power lines may look like trails, so confusion may result.

Another option is to have a custom map printed by going to a kiosk in an outdoors store (there are currently two dozen map machines just in Colorado). Several online companies, such as MyTopo.com (http://mytopo.com), Topozone (http://topozone.com), and Trails.com (http://trails.com), offer custom maps delivered to your door.

Kiosk and Internet maps will be printed on waterproof paper in sizes ranging from 13 by 18 inches to 26 by 36 inches (and even 36 by 44 inches or 36 by 50 inches, although these are too big for field use). Because such maps are seamless, a custom $15 map can be cheaper than purchasing several paper maps for a single trip, and they are very durable. The main draw-back to custom commercial maps is that you cannot include your own trails, notes, and symbols.

No matter how you print the maps, be certain they are the proper scale if you use map tools, such as rulers or a compass. If you reduce the size of the map to make it fit on a page, the printed scale will not be accurate.

Paper Maps

Although you can purchase digital topo maps for the entire United States, there is still much to be said for standard paper maps. For starters, many people don't have access to computer technology, and going digital can be expensive.

Many outdoors enthusiasts own USGS paper maps that are still quite serviceable after two or three decades in the collection—they earn a sentimental value after a rewarding trip—whereas you're lucky if a computer pro-gram is usable five years after purchase. Typically, for mapping software, there is no upgrade available between major versions, so if you have version 2.5 and want the features of version 3.0, you must pay full price again. Even if you don't upgrade your software, CDs are destined to go the way of floppy disks, so computers in the future probably won't read them.

For those interested in history, older maps some-times contain valuable information (e.g., the location of ghost towns, Indian ruins, and pictographs) that was removed in later versions. You may have to visit a state or university library to get copies.

Off-the-shelf commercial maps, such as the National Geographic Trails Illustrated series, can be a good choice for backcountry travel in many national parks. These seamlessly condense multiple 7½′ USGS maps onto dual-sided waterproof paper. While these maps are convenient, their scale varies depending upon the size of the park, so they may not offer adequate detail in large parks such as Glacier and Yosemite.

For Colorado, Trails Illustrated provides a series that covers most of the mountain region at 1:50,000.

However, no other state received this treatment. Commercial paper maps are the norm in most other countries.

Then, of course, there's the real thing: genuine U.S. government–issue 7½′ topographic maps printed on 21-by-27-inch paper sheets. All other maps described above are based on these, and just about everyone who works and plays in the outdoors is, or should be, familiar with them. Quite simply, you can't go wrong choosing the gold standard . . . but you can go off course if the trails have changed!

As of 2004, USGS maps list for $6 per map direct from the government. Other sizes of maps cost $7 each. Postage is $5 per order. Stores may charge a bit more because of low margins and high overhead; topo maps are more of a service than a big moneymaker for them.

Both Canada and Mexico have mapped their entire countries with 1:50,000 maps; larger-scale maps may be available in some areas (usually cities). At present, the paper maps are easier to obtain than digital versions, but this is changing.

There is one more option for high-quality 1:50,000 topo maps that cover a good portion of the planet's landmass; even more are available at 1:100,000. During the Cold War, the Soviet Union mapped all of Russia and Europe and much of Asia to a high standard of accuracy; before its collapse, it had once planned to map the entire globe to 1:25,000. These maps are now available to the public (see www.carto graphic.com), but the current price is $150 per sheet (there are 34,000 sheets for Russia, and even tiny Luxembourg requires 18 sheets) and the writing is in Cyrillic, so you have to *really* want them.

Purchasing Maps

Not too long ago, tracking down paper or digital maps for areas outside your region was a major hassle that could take many months. Now, thanks to the Internet, it is easy to go online and find maps for just about anywhere.

Certainly, your local outdoor shop is a good place to check for maps to areas within a couple hundred miles. You may also glean valuable information about current trail conditions, fishing reports, or avalanche warnings. But a shop in Maine isn't likely to stock maps of Colorado, and vice versa.

When you plan to travel farther afield, map stores are often your best bet. If you are fortunate to have one nearby, it's worthwhile to stop in—browsing is always educational since map stores usually stock a large assortment of maps from around the world.

Now, numerous map suppliers can be found online. Simply open a browser and type "topographic maps" into a search engine. Narrow the search by including the state or region that interests you.

You can also try commercial sites such as Maps .com, Maplink.com, Omnimap.com, Maptown.com, and Stanfords.co.uk.

Another option is to order maps direct from the USGS. The easiest method is to go to the USGS topo map website (http://topomaps.usgs.gov), because you can search by a number of parameters. If you don't have Internet access, call the toll-free number: 888-ASK-USGS.

A handy feature is the Geographic Names Information Server (GNIS), which lets you search the two million named features in the United States and Antarctica (http://geonames.usgs.gov/). For example, entering the location "Delicate Arch, Utah," will yield the name of the map it's found on (Big Bend) and the exact position. Links provided will take you to a digital map, a map of the watershed, and a satellite photo.

You can also learn fun facts, such as previous names for one of Utah's state symbols (seen on signs and centennial license plates), including Bloomers Arch, Chaps, Mary's Bloomers, Old Maids Bloomers, Pants Crotch, Salt Wash Arch, School Marms Pants, Schoolmarms Bloomers, and The Chaps. One can't help but wonder about the poor teacher who never married but had famous underwear.

If you are heading to Canada, finding the names of the proper maps online is also easy (see http://maps .nrcan.gc.ca). However, you must purchase them from a dealer; the government no longer sells direct.

Unless you have a good command of Spanish, it's easier to purchase topos of Mexico from a map store. The later editions have shaded relief, so they are both functional and pretty. The government does have online resources (www.inegi.gob.mx) and sells direct; don't get sticker shock—prices are in pesos.

Folding & Protecting Maps

USGS 7½′ maps are sold and usually mailed flat—that is, unfolded, rolled, and shipped in a tube. Nearly all commercial maps are prefolded.

Land navigators don't share the superstition of mariners that outlaws folding, though rolled paper maps do last longer than those that are folded. On the trail, you may occasionally see a map rolled around a fishing rod case. But a rolled map outdoors is a pain.

Before you start folding a map every which way, consider how it will be used.

With the type of compass that is most popular now, it is helpful to have one of the vertical margins of the folded map accessible on whatever part of the map you may be working with.

One way to achieve that is to fold the map horizontally in half (bring the two narrow ends together), printed side out. Then fold it vertically in half, again horizontally in half, and finally vertically in half. The map ends up about 5½ by 7 inches with the lower right corner, which contains the map name, on top. This easily fits in the pocket of a pack and can be refolded so that four sections nearest your location are handy.

Another method is to fold the map like a blueprint. First fold the map in half vertically (bring the two wide ends together) so that the printing faces inward. Then fold each half back in the other direction like an accordion; you now have a long, skinny map. Fold this into thirds so the lower right corner is on top. This gives you a 5½-by-9-inch map that packs well and shows more information.

Using the blueprint fold also reduces wear on maps because there are only six intersections rather than nine from the halving method. Paper maps usually give out first where creases cross.

Constant folding and refolding, abrasion inside a pack, and exposure to water are all rough on paper maps. If you want them to last, you must protect them.

One method is to laminate both sides with plastic in a heat press (now reasonably priced at business supply stores) or to encase the map in clear contact sheets (found at hobby shops) or plastic shelving paper (hardware stores). Laminated maps are indestructible but heavy and difficult to fold.

Or you can coat paper maps with a waterproof treatment such as Map Seal; some use Thompsons Water Treatment, but it may yellow the maps somewhat. These coatings are effective but tend to make the paper stiff.

There are some nifty transparent, waterproof map cases on the market. These are highly recommended for sea kayaking and whitewater canoeing or rafting trips but are probably overkill for backpacking unless you're in a very wet region. Some have a lanyard to carry the map dangling from your neck, which may be useful for rescue personnel.

The simplest and cheapest map case is a gallon-size Ziploc freezer bag, which very nicely fits a 7½′ map with the blueprint fold. Four panels of the map (a combined 10.5 by 18 inches) can be viewed at one time while staying clean and dry. Refold the map so panels you need are exposed, insert it sideways into the bag, then zip the bag closed, making sure to squeeze all the air out. When one bag gets too ratty for map use, you can demote it to a refuse bag and use a new one.

3.

Distance from the Map

We have agreed that maps show land areas greatly reduced in size. But how much reduced?

That will depend on how large a land area the map shows and, much less, on the size of the map; much less, because map sizes don't differ as much as the areas to be mapped.

A map used to teach in a classroom is perhaps 8 feet wide; the double-page map in this book is about as many inches wide. They differ by a factor of twelve.

The world is, in very round figures, 25,000 miles (40,000 kilometers) around the equator; New York City is about 20 miles (32 kilometers) wide from east to west. If you wanted to map both, and used the same reduction, the map of the world would have to be 1,250 times wider than the one of New York, which is obviously impractical. The major thoroughfares of New York City could be reasonably well shown on a double page of this book. The same rate of reduction would make a map of the world almost as wide as the lengths of three football fields.

You have lived with maps of about the same size—folded road maps and maps in an atlas or on a computer screen, for instance—all your life. Such maps must have different rates of reduction, or to use a shorter term, different *scales*.

You may have planned a trip to the West Coast on a map of the United States showing only the major highways and cities. For side trips, or as you approached your destination, for more detailed information you would have used a map that showed only California, or perhaps only Southern California. Then, to find the best approach to your aunt's place in Redondo Beach, you should have switched—or wished you had switched—to a map of Los Angeles.

To show the roughly 3,000 miles (about 4,800 kilometers) from coast to coast, the publishers of your road atlas shrank the distance by a factor of 9 million to about 21 inches (53 centimeters). The scale of that map would be described as 1:9,000,000.

That scale makes 1 inch on the map equal to 9,000,000 inches in the landscape (about 142 statute miles). It makes 1 centimeter on the map equal to 9,000,000 centimeters in the landscape (exactly 90 kilometers).

On your trip to the West Coast, when you saw the mountains, you just had to take a side trip. Perhaps to the less-used western portion of Rocky Mountain National Park. On the map of the United States you can barely find the park. So you switch to a map of Colorado.

On that map, the 77 almost-straight miles from Burlington (near the Kansas border) to Limon (where the road to Colorado Springs peels off) measure about 3½ inches. The scale works out to 1:1,400,000.

The map of greater Los Angeles, which shows most through streets, is drawn on a scale of 1:300,000. (One mile equals about ¼ inch; 1 kilometer, about 3 millimeters.)

Many people get confused when they hear or read about small-scale or large-scale maps.

A small-scale map shows a large area (such as the United States) with little detail—showing large features only; the figure following the "1:" is large (for example, 9,000,000). Obviously, each of the above statements is the other way around on a large-scale map. This may help you remember the facts:

Small-scale map	Large-scale map
Number after 1:–*large*	Number after 1:–*small*
Area covered–*large*	Area covered–*small*
Large features only	*Small* features shown

If life has taught you that things are often the reverse of what you expected, that's the way to remember it.

Mathematically inclined readers will have already realized that the scale of a map can be just as easily expressed as a fraction: $\frac{1}{9,000,000}$, $\frac{1}{300,000}$, and so on.

For hiking, skiing, canoeing, and other activities that take us perhaps as far in one day as an automobile might take us in a quarter hour or less, we need maps on much larger scales than even the map of greater Los Angeles.

You already know that we'd use topographic maps for these activities, maps that show the ups and downs of the terrain by contour lines. Such maps in the United States are mainly on several different scales.

For maximum detail, the generally available largest scale is either 1:24,000 or 1:25,000. That makes 1 inch equal to exactly 2,000 feet, the scale of the most popular 7½′ topo quads of the contiguous states.

Metric countries unimpeded by miles and inches have no reason to use that scale. They use 1:25,000, which makes 1 kilometer equal to exactly 40 millimeters. You'll find this scale used on Canadian and European maps, as well as some maps of Alaska. The detail and the area that can be shown on a given sheet size are, of course, virtually the same with these two scales. The second set of scales used on U.S. topographic maps is 1:63,360. A statute mile equals exactly 5,280 feet, or 63,360 inches. On a map on the scale of 1:63,360, 1 mile equals exactly 1 inch. That is the scale of most topographic quads in Alaska.

Countries on the metric system don't have any interest in statute miles and so do not use this scale. Their nearest equivalent is 1:50,000, one-half the 1:25,000 scale, making 1 kilometer exactly 20 millimeters on the map. You'll run across that scale on

European hiking maps and Canadian topo maps. About 10 percent of the counties in the United States are mapped at 1:50,000, so these can be great topo maps if you stay within the political boundaries—it's a good size for general outdoor purposes.

You may like the metric 1:100,000 series topo maps even better for activities where you cover a lot of ground. They cover four times the area of the 1:50,000 maps—30′ latitude by 60′ (1°) longitude. So a mile is ⅝ inch (16 millimeters), and these maps are much better suited for getting your location from distant mapped features. It also makes an emergency hiking map, say for an area you hadn't planned to visit. And it's a good scale for bicycle touring. Another 10 percent of the counties in this country are mapped at 1:100,000 so these may be worth checking too.

The scale of 1:250,000 is used on another series of topographic maps and is tied to an international reference system; each map covers 1° of latitude and 2° of longitude (3° in Alaska). On that scale a mile becomes ¼ inch (6 millimeters), which is too small for actual hiking but a good size for planning your approach or an extended trip that would spill over several larger-scale sheets. It's also a useful map for identifying distant mountains, lakes, and settlements that are well off your actual hiking map. Such distant landmarks can sometimes help you find out where you are.

Summary of Map Series

A good way to visualize all the different U.S. topographic maps would be to superimpose samples of each series on the map of a state. Let's use Colorado, not only because our map is from that state, but because Colorado has such a nice regular shape. It reaches from latitude 37°N to 41°N, and from longitude 102°03′W to 109°03′W. That's exactly 4° latitude by 7° longitude.

Each of the large quadrangles (1° latitude and 2° longitude) in Figure 3.1 shows one of the state's topographic maps on the scale of 1:250,000. It takes, as you

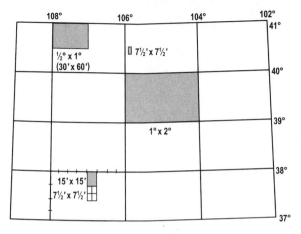

Figure 3.1 Topo map areas for the state of Colorado.

can see or calculate, sixteen of these maps to cover the state of Colorado, with half of each of the four western-most maps overlapping into Utah.

The smaller quadrangle at the top is a 1:100,000 quadrangle that covers ½° latitude by 1° longitude (or 30' by 60' as they are commonly indexed).

The next-smaller-size quadrangles represent the 15' by 15' 1:63,360 topographic maps used in Alaska: 1 inch equals 1 mile. You can see that it would take thirty-two of these maps to cover the area of one 1:250,000-scale map.

The smallest quadrangles represent the popular 7½' by 7½' topo maps on the 1:24,000 scale. (In Puerto Rico the scale would be 1:20,000.) The one near the top of Figure 3.1 shows the relation in size to the 1:250,000-scale maps. It takes 128 of the larger-scale maps to cover the area of the smaller-scale map. The small quadrangles at the lower left of the figure show the relation of the 7½' by 7½' maps to the 15' by 15'. It takes four 1:24,000 topo quads to cover the same area as one of the 1:63,360 maps. This is the most detailed series available. Don't let Figure 3.1 and what you just read mislead you into thinking that the map covering the largest area is large in paper size and the one cover-

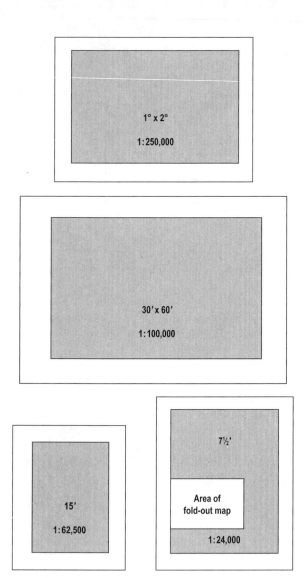

Figure 3.2 Relative sizes of topo maps.

ing the smallest area is small. All four maps in the different series are similar in dimensions, as shown in Figure 3.2. (Actually the 30′ by 60′ map is the largest, the 15′ by 15′ map the smallest.)

Distance from the Map

The similarity of size is no accident. A 5-foot-wide map is a nuisance to handle on a desk; on a mountain it would threaten to kite off, taking you with it.

When you purchase a digital map collection, you have the option of many different scales. The software can render the map at full scale (1:24,000), zoom back to 1:50,000, and even further back to 1:62,500, like the old 15′ maps that are no longer produced in the Lower 48. You can also zoom in to 1:12,500, but this merely magnifies the image without adding detail. The map software also may include 1:100,000 series maps that can also be zoomed.

Measuring Distances

Maps let you find the distance between any two mapped points, usually more accurately than any of us will ever need.

Anybody can learn in a few minutes how to measure distances on maps accurately. But one-tenth of a mile hardly ever matters. What counts is that you don't make a gross mistake, but if you do, you notice it before your party has to sleep on scree.

The way to avoid mistakes, or to catch them, is to get a feel for the scale of the map you are using (see Figure 3.3). That's not difficult. You probably use only one scale on any one day—say, a 1:50,000 topo map. You may have become bored by all the figures about scales in the past few pages and forgotten that on these maps 1 mile is almost exactly 1¼ inches.

If you were raised using the American standard system of measurement, that's all you need. After measuring 4 miles on the map, for instance, think: "Does that look like 5 inches?" If it does, it is probably right. Most of us can tell 5 inches from 4 or 6 inches, or at least get suspicious enough to double-check.

If you grew up using the metric system and think of distances in kilometers, you have to remember that 20 millimeters represent 1 kilometer on 1:50,000 maps. You know you've goofed if you measured what looks like much more or much less than 9 centimeters.

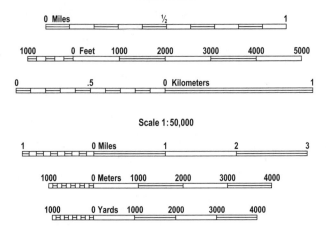

Figure 3.3 Graphic scales from the United States and Canada.

You can test yourself. On our map, for example, 1 mile is 2⅝ inches (2½ inches is close enough), and 1 kilometer is 42 millimeters (40 millimeters is close enough).

How far is it on the Ute Trail from the Fairview Curve (bottom of the map, near the center) to Milner Pass? Just looking at it, wouldn't you say about 2 miles (or 3 kilometers)?

You can get the necessary base numbers for miles or kilometers in inches or millimeters from Table 3.1. On 1:100,000 maps 1 kilometer is exactly 1 centimeter (0.1 mm). That's easily remembered, and not just because it's simple. It has to be so: 1 kilometer equals 1,000 meters, and 1 meter equals 100 centimeters. So 1 centimeter times 100,000—the scale of the map— equals 1 kilometer.

All other metric equivalents come easy after that: 1:50,000 means 2 centimeters per kilometer, 1:25,000 means 4 centimeters, 1:250,000 works out to 4 millimeters, and so on.

This isn't to say you should eyeball distances. Just check your measurements that way.

Table 3.1 Distance equivalents for commonly used scales*

		1 statute mile equals about:		*1 kilometer equals about:*	
Scale	*Maps*	*Inches*	*Millimeters*	*Inches*	*Millimeters*
Hiking maps					
1:20,000	Puerto Rico 7½′	3⅛	80	2	50†
1:24,000	**7½′ quads**	**2⅝**	**67**	**1⅝**	**42**
1:25,000	Metric maps	2½	64	1⅝	40†
1:50,000	Metric maps	1¼	32	¾	20†
1:63,360	Alaska 15′	1†	25	⅝	16
Planning maps					
1:100,000	U.S., metric	⅝	16	⅜	10†
1:250,000	U.S., metric	¼	6½	5/32	4†

*The most commonly used U.S. map is in boldface.
†Exactly.

To help with measurements, the U.S. maps discussed have graphic scales in both American standard and metric units. Foreign maps most likely use only metric units. Then you have a choice: you can learn to live with kilometers, as some travelers adapt to the local beer price in local currency; or you can convert units, as other travelers do. A kilometer is about six-tenths (actually 0.621) of a statute mile. One mile is about 1.6 (actually 1.609) kilometers.

Using metric 1:25,000-scale maps will seem very simple if you are used to the 7½′ series, which is on the scale of 1:24,000. The two scales are identical as far as hiking or skiing is concerned. The difference is only 4 percent of the distance.

Actually, the difficulty of switching from American standard to metric units is mostly in the user's mind. You could use 1:100,000 U.S. topographic maps for planning or identifying distant features of the landscape, only to find at the end of the summer that the map is all metric. You may not have noticed, because you simply used the graphic miles and feet scales, and perhaps the section lines.

You are not likely to use a map of that scale for figuring out how steep a trail is. So you never noticed that the contours were 50 meters apart. A conversion table on the map itself will tell you the equivalent in feet (164 feet).

Basic Measuring Techniques

How can you bring the distance between two points down to the scale at the bottom of the map?

There are several solutions.

One is to take a twig, scrap of paper, or finger and measure that. You may find that spreading your thumb and index finger creates a span that is by chance roughly 5 miles on the 1:50,000 map you are using. Then you can measure off 5 miles in any direction you like.

Or try this. Say the problem is to find the distance from where you left your car near the buildings straddling squares 7 and 12 to where the Red Mountain Trail joins the road along the Grand Ditch. Simply break a match, or a pine needle, so it's ½ mile long on the scale. Then weasel it around all the corners of the trail and get six times and a bit. The distance is therefore about 3 miles plus, or call it 3¼ miles.

The lanyard on your compass isn't just for wearing it around your neck. That red cord is also handy for measuring convoluted trails. Simply lay it over the approximate course, then straighten and measure using the map scale.

Maybe you've seen a gadget that you wheel over the map and that magically adds up all the distances you have pushed it. These gadgets work fine on a chart table. On a map that has been folded and now is balanced on your left knee they leave much to be desired.

The newer digital map measurers can calibrate the scale of any map to give you direct readings without any math. While handy at times, a measurer isn't worth carrying in the pack—data from digital maps are far superior.

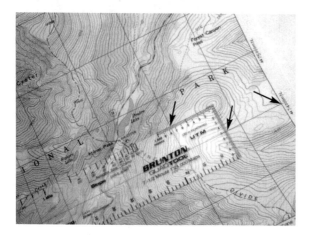

Figure 3.4 The Brunton Quad Tool ($15) is handy for working with maps.

There are two tools, however, that are useful in map work; both are inexpensive. The first is a 12-inch (30-centimeter) transparent ruler. The second is a magnifier.

The transparent ruler. A dime-store plastic ruler will suffice, but the commercial map rulers have useful scales for different maps and measuring slope angles (see Figure 3.4). You'll find multiple uses in navigation work for such a map ruler, since they are easier to use than the tiny scales on a compass.

It isn't often that we deal with straight-line distances, but when we do, rulers are an easy way to pick them off the map and convert them to the graphic scale of your choice (miles, feet, kilometers).

You may be opposed to the metric system, for whatever reason. But there is a way of taking advantage of the metric edge of the ruler without adopting the metric system, or what scientifically is called the *Système International.* Unless you are confident reading sixteenths and thirty-seconds of an inch—perhaps from cabinet-making or some other hobby or profession—you'll find this method faster and less error prone.

The numbers 1 to 30 on the 12-inch rule indicate centimeters. But you don't care about that. Each centimeter is divided into ten parts. For easy reading, every fifth unit—we might as well call them millimeters, although you don't have to—is marked by a longer line.

That makes counting the small divisions easy. They run from 0 at the lower numeral through 1, 2, 3, and 4 to the longer mark; then come 6, 7, 8, and finally 9 just before the next higher numeral.

Few people strictly count marks. Without much thought they call the mark to the left of the longer mark 4; to the right 6; to the left of the next numeral 9; and so on.

You can suit yourself about what to call the result of your measurement. You could call it 5.4 or 5.6 (with or without adding "centimeters"). Or perhaps 54, 56, or 58 (with or without "millimeters" added).

Transfer the marks to the graphic scales, say the miles scale. On a 1:24,000 map, your 54 "whatevers" will measure $\frac{8}{10}$ mile.

You don't have to read the metric scale at all if you don't want to; just keep the nail of your index finger (or thumb) on the mark when you move the ruler to the scale.

A twig picked up on the spot could be used in the same way. But for compass work it won't do. You'll soon see why.

The magnifier. Nothing elaborate is needed, but a magnifier can be a great help in, say, counting contour lines. Sometimes a pocket magnifier can save you digging out your reading glasses (just wait, kids), exchanging them for the sunglasses you were wearing, and reversing the whole process.

You may want to test yourself. Where the Red Mountain Trail meets the Grand Ditch, near the little pond, do you see from left to right a thin brown line, the blue of the ditch, two parallel black lines (the road), the dashes marking the trail, and a heavier brown line?

Many modern compasses have a magnifier molded into the base. Held a little distance from the map, it'll do the trick. Even if your compass is so equipped, you may want to carry a magnifier for observing the details of flowers or butterflies.

Here's another method of getting trail distances on a mapped trail even if the graphic scale isn't showing. First, find a straight section of a trail on your map. On it measure ½ mile (or ½ kilometer, depending on your persuasion). Then count the dashes in that stretch (your magnifier may help).

Say you get 18 dashes to the ½ mile. Even if the section of trail is not straight—how often is that?—if you count 72 dashes between two points, they are about 2 miles apart.

UTM Grids

Not surprisingly, the method for finding distance on most United States topographic maps is somewhat tilted toward miles. And most navigators are used to stating position with latitude and longitude in degrees, minutes, and seconds.

But there is an even more convenient system for estimating distance and designating locations. As mentioned earlier, USGS 1:24,000 topos have thin blue tick marks in all four margins that indicate exactly 1 kilometer. This is for an international map reference system, called the Universal Transverse Mercator (UTM) grid.

Some 7½′ maps have the UTM grid printed in black ink; however, these are the exception. Most will require drawing the grid by hand to effectively use the UTM system. For best results, use a straight-edge ruler with a cork backing (prevents slipping and smudging) and a fine-point pen with waterproof ink or mechanical pencil. Each map requires twenty-five lines, so the process to grid several maps can be tedious. Fortunately, with digital maps it takes just a few mouse clicks to have the UTM grid appear on maps you print out (blue ink stands out better).

When a map has a UTM grid, estimating distance becomes a simple process: just count the squares.

If your route happens to be east-west or north-south, you only have to add up the squares and fractions at each end of the trek, and you have your distance in kilometers. Multiply by 0.6 to get mileage.

If your route should cross the sections diagonally, say from northeast to southwest, it helps to know that the diagonal of each square is about 1.4 kilometers. That means seven sections traversed diagonally are nearly 10 kilometers long.

Trails usually don't follow these simple courses. But an askew trail will have to be between the limits of the shortest (1.0 kilometer) and the longest (1.4 kilometers) straight line through any one square. For ten squares that might be between 10 and 14 kilometers. That's close enough for a first guess; 12 kilometers may be a reasonable estimate for rough planning.

UTM Position

The UTM grid really comes into its own when used with a GPS unit. Because this is a decimal system based on units of ten, it is easy to estimate position within a grid square and convert that to a number. No more counting up to sixty and then starting over as you do with seconds and minutes.

Examine the full 7½′ sheet that contains our fold-out map and you'll find near the right bottom corner a blue tick mark labeled [4]35^{000m}E.

This is called the *easting*. The blue mark to the left is labeled simply with a small 4 and a larger 34 (called the *principal digits*). The blue mark left of that has a small 4 and large 33, and each subsequent mark decreases by one.

On maps and in guidebooks, the coordinates are usually printed with superscripts and bold text to help make reading easier. But this isn't necessary when you jot them down and isn't possible when you enter them into a GPS unit. Thus, 43500E is the same as [4]35^{000}E.

Close to the left top corner you'll find a mark labeled [44]83^{000m}N.

This is the *northing*. Each evenly spaced tick below it decreases by one. See the pattern? Move either east or north and numbers get bigger; head in the opposite directions, and the numbers get smaller.

Distance from the Map

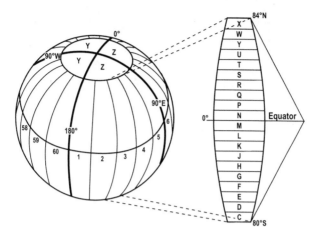

Figure 3.5 UTM grid of the world.

To make this whole thing work, the globe is divided into sixty vertical slices, called *zones*, that are 6° of longitude wide–rather like slicing an orange. The International Date Line (longitude 180°) in the Pacific forms the border of Zone 1 and Zone 60 (see Figure 3.5). On the opposite side of the planet, the prime meridian (longitude 0°), which runs through Greenwich, England, is the border of Zones 30 and 31. (The "Greenwich Meridian" was drawn by royal astronomer Sir George Airy in 1851 and agreed upon as a world time standard in 1884.)

To keep all numbers positive, the center of each zone (called a *central meridian*) is assigned ^{5}**00**^{000m}**E**. The kilometers count down from there, heading west until the next zone is reached. The minimum easting will range from 160,000 at the equator to 465,000 at 84° North, where the UTM system stops. Going east from the meridian, the kilometers are added until the next zone is reached; maximum eastings are 834,000 at the equator and 515,000 up in the Arctic.

The explanation at the bottom left of the map tells us we are in Zone 13. The contiguous United States extends from Zone 10 in Washington to Zone 19 in Maine (Russia spans twenty-seven zones!). (See Figure 3.6.)

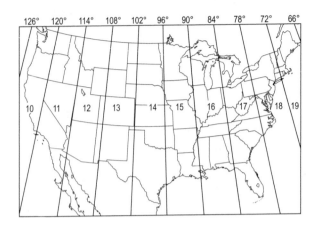

Figure 3.6 UTM zones of the United States.

The Fall River Pass map we are using tells us that the right side is about 65 kilometers (just over 40 miles) west of the meridian for Zone 13 (500,000 − 435,000 = 65,000 meters).

The northing is simply determined by counting the meters up from the equator, starting at 0. Thus the top edge of the map is 4,483,000 meters (2,784 miles) north of the equator.

For the Southern Hemisphere, the equator is assigned 10,000,000 and the northings count down as you head south; this means that you don't have to deal with negative numbers. So the summit of Aconcagua at $^{63}\mathbf{88}^{000m}\mathbf{N}$ is 3,612 kilometers (2,244 miles) south of the equator (10,000,000 − 6,388,000 = 3,612,000 meters).

Where the UTM system does get a little odd is at the border of two zones. For example, you are hiking east on the Navajo Basin Trail to climb spectacular Wilson Peak near Telluride, Colorado. In a matter of feet, when you step from the Dolores Peak to the Mount Wilson quad, your easting changes from 120763966 to 130236036. But at this point, you are well above tree line at 12,250 feet and probably thinking more about the incredible view (or impending storm).

The UTM grid is also problematic in the far north. The grid was modified to keep southwest Norway in the same zone (32) as the rest of the country. Even closer to the pole, the grid was modified to keep the Svalbard islands in two zones rather than spread among five.

Applying UTM

Using the UTM grid (and the NAD 27 datum), Peak 11961 on our map, just below the word "PARK," has the full coordinates: $13^{04}32^{792}E$ $^{44}74^{306}N$.

Since we are operating on a large-scale map, which makes the zone and first two digits a given for everything on the map, the coordinates can be abbreviated (in this case by dropping the 13^{04} of the easting and the ^{44} of the northing and then rounding up). The key is that the UTM position always contains an even number of numbers; the first half are the easting, the second half the northing.

Therefore, the modified coordinate 3279 7431 narrows the position of the peak's summit to a 10-meter-by-10-meter square. Even the simplified coordinate 328 743 puts you within a 100-meter square box, which is certainly close enough to locate the summit, and 33 74 gets you within a square kilometer.

Under the old system, Peak 11961 lies at a latitude and longitude of 40°25'06"N 105°47'32"W. Or, stated in decimal form, 40°25.1'N 105°47.5'W (or 40.418°N 105.792°W).

To find the distance from Peak 11961 to Milner Pass, whose UTM coordinate is 3116 7448, you can use simple subtraction (3,279 − 3,116 = 163), showing that the pass is almost exactly 1.63 kilometers (1 mile) due east of Peak 11961. The calculations needed to solve the same problem using the latitude-longitude coordinates (40°25'12"N 105°48'41"W), however, are mind-boggling.

All of this is greatly simplified by using a map with a predrawn UTM grid and a grid tool, called a roamer scale, found on some compasses.

Figure 3.7 Using a UTM roamer scale.

To find the coordinates, just place the upper right corner of the grid tool over a point. Then add the numbers shown on the roamer scale to the UTM numbers in the margin. (See Figure 3.7.)

Other Grids

The U.S. Military Grid Reference System (MGRS) is simply a variation of the UTM grid system, a different way of expressing the same thing. It is an option on many GPS units.

This system divides the globe into twenty rows or bands that are each 8° of latitude high (the northern-most band is 12° high). The system starts at the equator (0°) with the letter *N*. As you move north, the letters ascend toward the end of the alphabet; as you move south, the letters descend toward the beginning of the alphabet. To avoid confusion with numbers, the letters *I* and *O* have been omitted.

Under this system, our Fall River Pass map falls in grid zone 13T. Since the northing already tells you how far you are from the equator, this lettering system is just a fast reference to the part of the zone you are

in. Most civilians will not bother with designating latitude bands.

The MGRS takes this lettering scheme a step further by subdividing each grid zone into squares that
are 100 kilometers wide. Each square has a two-letter
designation, such as "DQ" for our map, but you won't
find these letters on USGS maps (most mapping software or a GPS unit will tell you if desired).

In military parlance, Peak 11961 is found at coordinate 13TDQ32797431. Notice that the last eight
numbers are the same as in our UTM coordinates
above. The "D" replaces "04" on the easting and the
"Q" replaces "44" on the northing.

The UTM grid covers most of the landmasses on
the planet but stops at 84° North and 80° South. If you
visit the Arctic or Antarctic, then you will likely use the
Universal Polar Stereographic (UPS) grid system.

This UPS grid works the same as UTM, but the
Antarctic is divided into A and B sections, while the
Arctic is divided into Y and Z.

Sections & Section Numbers

Should you choose not to use the UTM grid system,
your maps may already have another handy method of
guesstimating distance and even establishing location.

Many topo maps and most national forest maps
show mysterious red squares: land sections as originally surveyed for the archaic township and range system (see Figure 3.8). Each was intended to be as close
to 640 acres as possible; that is, 1 mile by 1 mile. The
system covers most of central and western United
States (missing are the original thirteen states, Hawaii,
Kentucky, Tennessee, Texas, and West Virginia). Although not accurate for position, the system is commonly used for defining areas and is often referred to
on real estate documents.

On our map, the sections labeled 12 and 7 are
good examples; so are sections 18 and 13 on the complete map. Sections 1 and 6 are odd sized, the result of
mistakes in the original survey. Many such sections are

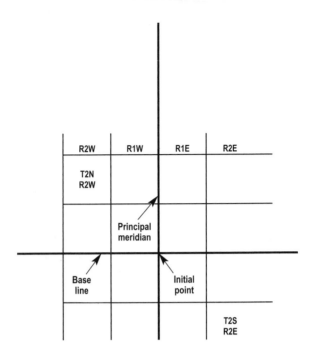

Figure 3.8 Numbering of townships and ranges.

in fact not square, but rectangular or odd shaped. If you had bought the section that includes Shipler Mountain or Hitchens Creek, for instance, you would have legally acquired more than 900 acres.

Counting section grids, like counting UTM squares, is a quick way to estimate distance, but in miles instead of kilometers. This method is particularly handy for Americans using the 1:100,000 series maps, which, except for the red section lines, are in metric.

Section Lines

Some readers may have wondered about the numbering of the sections on our map. Why does section 1 border on sections 6 and 12, for example?

Congress ordered it that way in 1785 upon recommendation of a committee headed by Thomas Jefferson.

Somewhat simplified, the scheme is as follows. At a given initial point two lines are established. One, running north-south, is the principal meridian of the area to be surveyed; the other, running east-west, is the base line.

Additional lines are drawn 6 miles apart and parallel to the principal meridian (range lines). Other lines are drawn also 6 miles apart but parallel to the base line (township lines). Townships are numbered starting from the base line, both north and south. Ranges are numbered from the principal meridian, both east and west.

That explains the red figures near the top left corner of our map.

The Hitchens Gulch section lies in Township 5 North (T5N), in Range 76 West (R76W). The section containing Shipler Mountain also lies in Township 5 North, but in Range 75 West (R75W).

Each one of the 6-square-mile areas—also called townships, to confuse you—is divided into 1-square-mile sections, as we already know. The numbering mandated by Congress so long ago starts at the northeast corner with 1, going west and snaking back and forth to end with 36 in the southeast corner.

6	5	4	3	2	1
7	8	9	10	11	12
18	17	16	15	14	13
19	20	21	22	23	24
30	29	28	27	26	25
31	32	33	34	35	36

That explains the numbering of sections on our map: 1, 12, and 13 are the easternmost sections of R76W; 6, 7, and 18 are the westernmost sections of R75W.

Someday, when you aren't certain where you are—a polite way of saying lost—you may see a yellow sign with black numbers nailed to a tree. One extra nail marks the section corner where you are standing.

To the right of the La Poudre Pass Trail, about halfway up our map, the sign would read 5N 76W and the nail would be at the right edge between the figures 1 and 12.

The numbering scheme is admittedly not the simplest. Many maps give the numbers of all thirty-six sections, and those who work with them frequently, surveyors and foresters, for example, become well familiar with them. To keep maps uncluttered, sometimes only the four corner sections (1, 6, 31, and 36) are numbered. Once you remember the snaking, you can reconstruct all the other numbers. Your pencil stub may be needed here.

Section numbers, without any further identification of township and range, are often a handy way to refer to a spot on the map. A member of your party may borrow your map and ask, "Where are we now?" He knows, of course, that he is trudging up the West Fork. So the answer "In section 32" is enough; the rest is obvious. That's more elegant than saying "Somewhere within a finger north of the letter *F* in 'Fork.'" While less precise than a UTM square, it still gets you in the ballpark.

Estimating Travel Time

Great accuracy in measuring distances on the map makes for good trivia but has limited practical value. With mapping software, you can determine that the Red Mountain Trail is 3.181 miles (5.119 kilometers) long from the parking lot to Grand Ditch. Dandy, but what you really want to know is if you have time to get there and back to the car.

A GPS unit can reveal your location within a 10-foot (3-meter) circle but is generally unreliable for estimating the round-trip time. Don't even bother wearing a pedometer—they're fine for an even pace on flat ground, like walking around town, but are wildly inaccurate on hilly, uneven trails.

So what it boils down to is this: although you can determine distances from maps or GPS units, what you really want to know is, how long will it take? And during the hike the question may be, how much longer?

The answers to such questions can be important.

For instance, the weather may be too awful to go on. "How far to where we can turn off and sit it out?" Or, early in the afternoon the question might be, "Will we make the planned campsite before dark, or should we look for a suitable spot now?"

What we need, then, is a formula to translate miles (or kilometers) from the map into hours on the trail.

Most people can plan on hiking 2 to 3 miles (about 3 to 5 kilometers) per hour on flat or mildly descending trails with a light to moderate load (less than 30 pounds, or 14 kilograms). This includes time for rest breaks and taking photos.

For each 1,000-foot (300-meter) rise, allow one extra hour. (Chapter 4 deals with measuring rise, descent, and steepness on the map.) For steeply descending sections of trails, add a half hour per 1,000 feet (300 meters).

These estimates have the beauty of simplicity and are easily remembered. (To keep them simple, meters are rounded; for example, 300 in place of 328.)

Consider a loop hike that leaves from the trailhead, follows the La Poudre Pass Trail, takes the Thunder Pass Trail (just above our cutout) to the Grand Ditch, where it heads back down valley to the Red Mountain Trail, bringing you back to the parking lot. It's about 12.7 miles (20 kilometers) with 2,290 feet (700 meters) of ascent and descent.

On flat ground, a hike of that length would take 4.2 to 6.3 hours. To this we'll add 2.3 hours for climbing to the Ditch. Maybe one more if you just came from sea level and aren't used to the thin air at 10,000 feet (3,000 meters). Add another 1.2 hours for the descent to the valley floor. So, the full circle should take between 8 and 10 hours.

You may find that these simple figures don't quite fit your style of hiking, skiing, or running. Time yourself on a few excursions and adjust the figures (rounded for convenience) to suit your progress.

You may find that with your usual pack weight, taking photographs, admiring the scenery, and retying your shoelaces, you cover only 1½ miles (2½ kilometers) per hour on the flat. If you've adopted ultralight hiking, your circuit could be twice as fast as the basic formula predicts (4 to 5 hours). A conditioned trail runner could do this loop in about 2 to 3 hours.

Perhaps you only need an extra hour for a 1,200-foot (350-meter) climb, which works out to be about 50 minutes for each 1,000 feet. If you are trail running, it may take only 30 minutes. If you are breaking trail through deep snow on backcountry skis, it may take 2 hours.

If you kept a rough log of past trips, or have an unusually sharp memory, and still have topo maps of the areas, you can work out your personal equation without putting on your boots.

An average pace for through-hiking the Appalachian Trail is 2.3 miles (3.7 kilometers) per hour plus one additional hour for each 700-foot (a bit more than 200-meters) rise. Add or subtract 15 percent depending on the condition of the trail.

Unfortunately, the condition of the trail cannot usually be read from the map. All backpackers can recall trail conditions that significantly slowed their progress: a pack trail out west with a creek on one side, a cliff on the other, and overlapping prints of horses' hooves all over; a stretch of pancake-flat Florida Trail section turned to thick mud through the Everglades with swamp on either side; a scramble down a talus slope where every step releases a mini-avalanche of rocks; in winter, traversing breakable crust with nothing underneath it, with or without skis . . . that 15 percent wouldn't begin to cover these situations.

After hiking several trails in a guide book, you can get a feel for the author's time estimates—sometimes off by 25 percent, one way or the other—and adjust your planning on future treks. Trail signs in the Alps, whether they are put up by alpine clubs or by local authorities, frequently give walking time, not distance. One soon learns to multiply posted times by one's personal factor.

Whatever formulas and corrections you choose, they serve a double purpose. They let you figure the total trail time and allow you to check your progress between mapped landmarks. At each landmark—peak, saddle, creek crossing, or whatever—you begin a new count to keep track of the distance traveled from that point.

Regarding overall time, it pays to overestimate. When you tell your party, "It'll take about 5 hours," the figure becomes etched in their minds and the "about" is forgotten. Better make it 6 hours in your announcement, even if you think you'll make it in 5.

Even when you don't have to fear mutiny, it is wise to overestimate when travel time is short, say, when you didn't get to the trailhead until noon. It's especially important in winter, when days are short.

Knowing the amount of daylight and even the time of sunrise and sunset can be invaluable to your planning. Some GPS units will calculate solar data for any location and date you desire. You can also find this information on the Internet (try the U.S. Naval Observatory, http://aa.usno.navy.mil/data, or http://sunrisesunset.com).

If neither option is available, Table 3.2 will help you estimate the hours of daylight. It covers only fall and winter; the rest of the year the time from sunrise to sunset is at least 12 hours. You'll find the approximate length of day (in hours and tenths of hours) on the line of the nearest date in the column of the nearest latitude. For a margin of safety, you can take the next greater latitude. (Table 12.2 provides the same information for southern latitudes.)

Example 1. Estimate the hours of daylight on November 15 at latitude 45°N.

Table 3.2 shows that on November 17 (closest day given) at latitude 45°N, the length of day is 9.5 hours. To estimate the hours of daylight at a latitude of 48°N, round up to the next nearest latitude, 52°, to get 8.7.

Table 3.2 Length of day in northern latitudes*

	Latitude					
Date	20°N	35°N	45°N	52°N	56°N	60°N
Sept. 21	12.1	12.2	12.3	12.4	12.4	12.5
Oct. 1	12.0	11.9	11.8	11.7	11.6	11.5
11	11.8	11.5	11.2	11.0	10.8	10.6
23	11.6	11.1	10.7	10.3	10.0	9.6
Nov. 4	11.4	10.7	10.1	9.5	9.1	8.6
17	11.2	10.3	9.5	8.7	8.1	7.4
26	11.1	10.1	9.2	8.3	7.6	6.8
Dec. 11	10.9	9.8	8.8	7.8	7.1	6.0
Jan. 16	11.1	10.1	9.2	8.3	7.6	6.8
Feb. 2	11.3	10.5	9.8	9.1	8.6	8.0
14	11.5	10.9	10.4	9.9	9.5	9.1
25	11.7	11.3	10.9	10.6	10.4	10.1
Mar. 8	11.9	11.7	11.5	11.3	11.2	11.1
18	12.1	12.0	12.0	12.0	12.0	12.0

*Time between sunrise and sunset is given in hours and tenths of hours; one-tenth of an hour equals six minutes.

You'll get a slightly more accurate result by using a compromise between the earlier and the later date when the difference between dates is large.

Example 2. Estimate the hours of daylight on February 7, latitude 52°N. February 2 has 9.1 hours of daylight, and February 14 has 9.9 hours—a difference of 48 minutes. The compromise value of 9.5 hours is closer to the actual value.

When planning your hike to take advantage of available daylight hours, don't forget to take into consideration preparation time needed at the trailhead and also time for setting up camp in the evening.

Distance from the Map

4.

Height
from the Map

You already know in a general way that the brown contour lines on topographic maps indicate elevations. Even without contour lines there are many points on topographic maps from which you can read the elevation directly.

Scattered across our map are X-marks with the letters *BM* and a numeral. *BM* stands for bench mark, a surveyor's vertical control station. The center of the cross indicates the exact location, and the numeral gives the elevation in feet (or in meters on metric maps).

The starting point for measuring elevations used to be called mean sea level. That's the level of the ocean after eliminating the effect of waves and tides.

The waves are easy to eliminate. You set up a recording gauge in a protected corner of a quiet harbor and surround the float that drives your recorder with a box in which a few holes admit the water but not the waves.

The effect of the tides is eliminated by averaging hourly observations of sea level for about nineteen years. After that time the positions of sun and moon, and with them the tides, repeat themselves.

That may be interesting, but it's useless for measuring elevations in Colorado unless you can bring the sea level to these mountains by geodetic surveying.

That, of course, is what has been done. The new starting point, the *datum,* of elevations on modern

United States topographic maps is called the National Geodetic Vertical Datum of 1927, a mean sea level adopted at that time.

You may have seen a round bronze disk set into the rock of a mountain peak. That was a bench mark. They are more common than mountain peaks. Every place in the contiguous United States is within 1 to 3 miles of a bench mark.

On our map they are all along the highway and the Grand Ditch.

They are not always as easy to see as on a mountain peak. They are placed, on purpose, where they are not likely to be disturbed. Surveyors and others with a need to know get the exact location from published data: so many feet west of the centerline of the road, for example, and so many feet north of somewhere else.

There are many more elevations printed on our map—on the peaks along the Continental Divide, for example.

You'll also see elevation figures for many section corners. Elevation is indicated on the map by an upright red cross. The elevation refers to the position of that marker.

Horizontal control stations are marked on maps by an equilateral triangle with a dot in the center indicating the exact location. (Sorry, there isn't one on our map.) An elevation is often given next to it, with or without the letters *BM*. Occasionally you'll see the abbreviation *VABM*, which stand for "vertical angle bench mark." That refers to a less accurate method of surveying (but still more accurate than we shall ever need).

Some elevation figures are printed in brown rather than black. That indicates the elevations, taken from an earlier map, have not been rechecked.

Lake and river elevations are given in either blue or black. There is no special significance in the choice of color.

All these symbols and conventions are not restricted to topographic maps; you'll find them on planimetric maps. Even road maps give the height of some passes, peaks, and lakes.

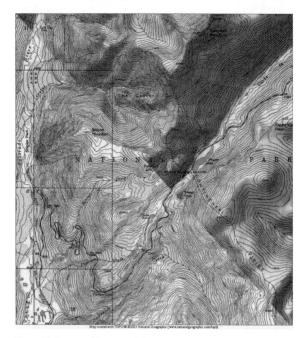

Figure 4.1 Topographic map with (upper right) and without (lower left) shading. The difference is even more striking in color.

You already know what makes topographic maps: contour lines. Before aerial photography and photogrammetry made maps with contour lines economical, shading and hachures—short lines drawn in the direction of the steepest slope, densest where the land was steepest—were used to convey the feel of the ups and downs of the land.

Some USGS contour maps are available with or without oblique shading, which adds a suggestion of a third dimension.

One is the already-mentioned map of Rocky Mountain National Park. Figure 4.1 shows an example of shaded relief and how it helps reveal the shape of the terrain.

The three-dimensional views from mapping software can be stunning—some can even drape the framework with aerial photos (see Figure 11.3).

Interesting though 3-D maps are for many purposes, for foot travel the regular topos are more useful. A printout of a 3-D view can be helpful for orienting yourself in the countryside, but standard maps are better for pinpointing your location.

Contour Lines

Don't feel bad if you can't picture the landscape by looking at the squiggly brown lines on topographic maps. Sight-reading contour lines is not a skill we are born with or can acquire without effort. And it has nothing to do with smarts. Most people have to work at it until one day it becomes as natural as driving a car.

A common way to learn this skill is to view a landscape in perspective and the same landscape on a map with contour lines. Let's try a different approach and build a map of some very simple shapes.

Pretend for a moment that the top sketch in Figure 4.2 is a volcanic island.

Now we'll make a map of it. The first contour line to be drawn is the zero elevation line, the coastline at mean sea level. Obviously, if the island is this simple, that contour line will be a circle—a circle that connects all points of zero elevation. We'll call it zero feet, but here and in the next paragraphs you could read it in meters just as easily.

Now imagine that global warming melts some of the polar ice caps and raises the sea level 100 feet. The new contour line will be another, smaller circle that connects all the points 100 feet above the original sea level.

Unfortunately, greenhouse gases continue to raise temperatures and some more ice melts, until the water has risen another 100 feet. The contour line will be a still smaller circle connecting all the points 200 feet above the original sea level.

Things really get bad and more ice melts. The water raises another 100 feet, and then another 100 feet, until it laps at the peak.

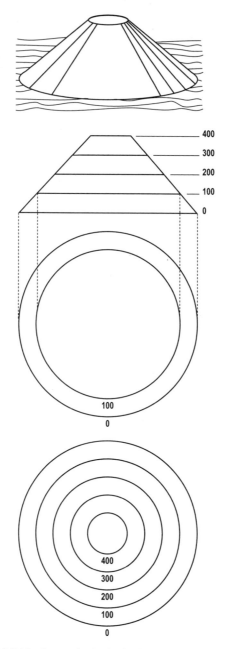

Figure 4.2 Raising the water level in 100-foot increments reveals the contours of a cone.

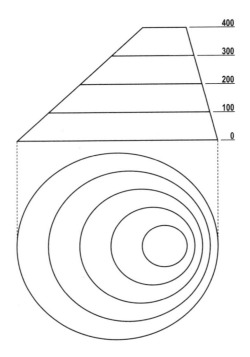

Figure 4.3 Contours of a tilted cone.

The contour line that connects all points 400 feet above the original sea level will be a very small circle.

The contour lines on a map can be thought of as an aerial view of such rings.

That last sentence is the key to the whole riddle of the brown squiggles. If you can see that, you are almost there.

To go the rest of the way, let's tilt the cone of the first experiment, as shown in Figure 4.3. You can see that the right edge in the drawing is now steeper than the left.

Again you start by drawing the shoreline (at mean sea level), then raise the water 100 feet at a time, drawing contours just as before. Instead of circles, they will form ellipses, like the figures your flashlight beam makes on the floor when you shine it at an angle rather than vertically.

By now, you are ready to deduce the first and most important rule about contour lines:

> Contours are closer together where the land is steep, farther apart where it is less steep.

Perhaps you found these mental experiments too elementary. There are no such mountains, at least not in Colorado—or are there?

Follow the Continental Divide from Milner Pass toward the bottom of our map. Does the first peak (unnamed, at 11,881 feet) remind you of the tilted cone and its rings seen from above?

Less than three-quarters of a mile away is Peak 11,961. Does it look familiar?

On our map, as on many 7½′ quads in the mountains, the contours are 40 feet (12 meters) apart. That corresponds to our raising the ocean 100 feet at a time.

The contour interval is printed right on the map, usually directly below the graphic scales.

Even when the map is folded or the bottom margin has been cut off, you can get the contour interval from the lines themselves.

Find two numbered contours on your map. They'll be heavy lines, called *index contours*. In the top right corner, you'll find one index contour labeled 10,800, and another—the label north of Poudre Lake—11,000. The interval between *index* contours is, therefore, 200 feet. Next, count the spaces between the two lines. There are five, so the contour interval is 200 ÷ 5, or 40 feet.

Maps that use 25-foot contour intervals have four spaces between index contours, 100 feet apart.

Not all maps of the 7½′ series use the 40-foot contour interval. In southern Florida, where the terrain is very flat, one contour would be in one county and the next one two quads away in the next. Instead, a 10-foot interval might be used.

Sometimes you must carefully check to see if elevations are increasing or decreasing. Often the blue color on the map is a quick aid. The Colorado River runs, generally, north to south on our map. Both banks, east and west of the floodplain, must be rising away from the river.

Poudre Lake and the Cache La Poudre River flowing out of it must also be low spots in their areas.

The area inside the last closed contour anywhere on a map leaves some doubt at times. Is the land still climbing, flat, or perhaps gently sloping?

The 11,881 and 11,961 peaks leave no doubt; each happens to be just one foot higher than the last contour. So the land, obviously, is not rising much.

If a lake is shown inside the last contour, it's a safe bet the land is dropping. Without such a lake, the drop would be shown on the map by one or more *depression contours*, which are contours sprouting short lines pointing downhill. Foreign maps may show a single arrow pointing down in this situation, much as an architect might show stairs leading to the basement.

It may help readers who still have trouble with the basic concept of contour lines to see how contours were mapped—with much effort—before photogrammetry became available.

A lot of points were surveyed. Their direction and distance from the stationary surveyor gave the location of the map points. The angle of his telescope together with the known elevation of the instrument gave the elevation of each point surveyed. That figure was written next to the point on the sheet.

Later, in the office, all the points with the exact elevation of a contour line, say 11,400 feet, were connected. Many points, of course, fell between contours. In drawing smooth curves the draftsman averaged higher and lower and drew the line between them. The process was similar to the way a meteorologist draws smooth isobars to fit the barometer readings from many stations.

Still confused?

Take a look at the Grand Ditch on our map, laid out near the 10,200-foot contour. This is built to gradually move water north while the river below flows south.

Height from the Map

To achieve this feat, the Grand Ditch is almost perfectly level with just a very slight gradient. From the lower left corner of the Fall River Pass quad to the gauging station at La Poudre Pass, the Grand Ditch measures 11.9 miles (19.1 kilometers) long (our cutout only shows 4.8 miles). The starting elevation is 10,280 feet (3,133 meters) and it reaches the Continental Divide at 10,180 feet (3,103 meters).

Now that you know the Grand Ditch is nearly horizontal, notice how it winds its way north. And, not coincidentally, the ditch parallels the brown contour lines on our map.

Perhaps you have seen a model of some mountain landscape made of layers of plywood. Such a model illustrates the way contour lines work. And it is much easier to make than a true relief.

First you transfer contour lines—enlarged—from a topographic map onto pieces of plywood. You may want to use only every other contour line or only index contours to make your job easier. You then cut the plywood along the lines with a jigsaw. (All contours curve back on themselves, unless they run off the edge of the map.) Then you assemble the cutouts one on top of the other, and you have your model.

A bit crude perhaps, but quick. You could use the layered model as an armature for a true relief map—just smear modeling clay on the steps with a putty knife to change them to smooth slopes.

You can find illustrations of the rule about contour spacing—close where the land is steep, far apart where it is almost flat—in many places on our map.

The best example is the Colorado River valley. Near the river the lines are far apart, indicating fairly flat land. On the west bank, especially in section 12, and on the east bank, especially in section 6, the map is brown with closely spaced contour lines.

Now look at Shipler Mountain in section 6. Find the nameless creek that runs into the Colorado. Look at the contours in the vicinity of that creek. You'll notice the otherwise rather smooth curves taking a sharp turn in toward higher elevations and then turning out again.

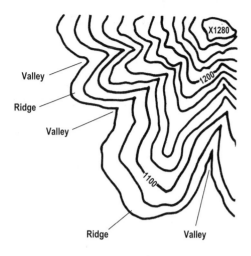

Valley

Ridge

Valley

1200

1100

Ridge   Valley

Figure 4.4 Contours of ridges and valleys.

That configuration is common at mountain creeks. Look, for example, at Lost Creek, which enters the Colorado just about opposite the unnamed creek. Or look at Squeak Creek in section 7.

Look at Shipler Mountain again. About a quarter-mile north of the source of the nameless creek begins a set of other, rather gentler, bends in the contours pointing to lower elevations. They indicate a ridge, a mountain spur.

We can now offer a second rule about contour lines:

In valleys, bends in contours point to higher elevations and are often V-shaped.

On ridges, bends in contours point to lower elevations and are often U-shaped.

Figure 4.4 illustrates that rule. But things are not always so simple. The ridge between the unnamed creek and Squeak Creek is a good example of U-shaped bends in the lower reaches above the road. But at the 10,600 contour and above the bends become rather

V-shaped; they still point downhill, so they can't belong to a valley. Look again at Squeak Creek at the same contour line and notice how it bends uphill.

You'll never see a creek running along the top of a ridge. But don't expect every valley to have its own creek, a mapped blue line.

There is a third generalization we can make about contour lines:

> Contour lines are always at right angles to the steepest slope.

Put a different way, a skier would say he or she skis at right angles to the fall line. For the benefit of nonskiers, that's not where the skier falls, spills, craters, sitzmarks, yard sales, or whatever. Rather, it is the line a smart grand piano on skis would choose to end its misery: the shortest way down. That would be the same direction the artist would have drawn his hachures to indicate the trend of the slope.

It helps some people visualize the shapes of mountains to think of lines perpendicular to the contour lines. See if that works for you. Start with the straight cone in Figure 4.2, then the tilted one in Figure 4.3, then look at different areas of our map. Start with some simple feature, say the west bank of the Colorado, then try the two unnamed peaks, and graduate with some highly irregular shape, such as Shipler Mountain as a whole.

Later, in Chapter 9, you will learn how that simple third rule may help you orient yourself even when the visibility is rotten.

Reading the Slope

Can we tell from a topo map how steep a trail is? Certainly.

Suppose a friend wanted to know how steep the Trail Ridge Road was between Fairview Curve and Milner Pass. You might talk your friend into accepting a figure starting just before the Phantom Creek crossing rather than from the curve. First you measure the distance with a string or mapping software and get about 2.8 miles. You then calculate the difference in elevation from the two bench marks: 10,758 at the top, 9,994 at the bottom—a difference of 764 feet. Divide the difference in elevation by the distance, and you get about 270 feet per mile on an average.

But using only bench marks on a topographic map is like using your hiking boots for doorstops. There are better uses for maps and boots.

Let's work some examples of measuring and calculating slope from contour lines.

Example 1. What is the slope of the Ute Trail, which we used to practice measuring distance in Chapter 3, between the Fairview Curve and Milner Pass (a distance of about 1.9 miles)?

The trail starts about one and a half contour intervals—roughly 60 feet—below the 10,200-foot index contour. Call it 10,140 feet. The last contour the trail touches, just before recrossing the road, is the one below the 10,800 index contour, the 10,760-foot level. (That checks nicely with the nearby bench mark elevation of the pass, 10,758 feet).

The trail rises 620 feet in about 1.9 miles. We can express that better in several ways. For example, 1.9 miles at 5,280 feet per statute mile equals 10,032 feet; that divided by 620 feet gives about 16. The trail rises, on the average, 1 foot in 16 feet, or 1 meter in 16 meters.

You can also divide the other way around, 620 ÷ 10,032, to get 0.06. A highway engineer would call it a 6 percent grade. The trail rises 6 feet in 100 feet, or 6 meters in 100 meters, and requires an extra 6 percent of force to maintain speed.

Yet another way to calculate slope is that used in Chapter 3 to estimate walking time—rise in feet per mile. To get that you divide 620 feet by 1.9 miles and get 326 feet per mile for an average.

Example 2. What is the average grade and foot-per-mile rise on the Red Mountain Trail, from where you left your car near the buildings at the eastern border of section 12 to where the trail joins the road along the Grand Ditch?

If you really want to learn the business, you should work that problem yourself, then check your answer against the figures that follow.

For distance you should get about 3¼ miles, as we did in Chapter 3. For the starting elevation, you probably used 9,040 feet (the stub end of the dirt road is right at that contour). The end of the trail here is above the 10,200 index contour but below the next one. Call it 10,220 feet. That makes the rise 1,180 feet.

The distance is 17,160 feet (3¼ miles at 5,280 feet per mile). Divide that by the rise and you get an average grade of 1:14.5 (i.e., a 1-foot rise for every 14.5 horizontal feet). Divide the other way and you get about 0.07, or a 7 percent average grade. The simplest calculation of all is the rise in feet per mile. Divide the rise by 3.25 miles, and you'll get about 360 feet per mile.

In contrast, the Grand Ditch drops 330 feet in 11.9 miles. Which means it has a 0.2 percent grade.

Example 3. What's the total rise on a beeline scramble from your car to the Grand Ditch, shortcutting the Red Mountain Trail? How steep is it?

The easiest way to answer these questions is to use digital mapping software. Simply select the measuring tool, click on the starting point, then click on the ending point. The information window will tell you distance and elevation gain among other trivia.

Assuming that you aren't hiking with your laptop computer, another simple way to solve the first question is to count spaces between contour lines you would cross on that climb. You can use that technique regardless of the angle at which you would cross the contours.

You'll find a magnifying glass and a pointer, say a pine needle, helpful in counting. You'll also save a lot of eyestrain by counting, where possible, by spaces between index contours and then multiplying the result by the number of intervals between index contours, here five.

There are four spaces to the first index contour; then five spaces between index contours; and finally about half a contour interval to the road that parallels the Grand Ditch.

You could figure four spaces of 40 feet, plus five times 200, plus 20 feet gives 1,180 feet. You could also figure 4 plus 5 times 5 plus ½ gives 29½ contour intervals of 40 feet, or 1,180 feet. (That, of course, is the same result as in Example 2, where we subtracted the elevation at the bottom from that at the top.)

The counting and calculations are easier than the scramble. The straight-line distance, as you can check, is only 0.7 mile.

That makes the rise close to 1,700 feet per mile, a steep 1:3 or 32 percent grade, overall.

But that average does not tell the whole story. After an easy start comes a 400-foot climb in a 600-foot distance, corresponding to a rise of 3,500 feet per mile.

How do you measure that?

With a digital mapping program, you just click the profile button and are presented a window showing a cross section of the slope. Moving the cursor reveals that this beeline hike starts off with a gentle 5 percent grade, steepens to 15 percent, then gets brutal with one section hitting a 42 percent grade before it relaxes to about 20 percent.

Measure the old-fashioned way by putting a ruler across the brownest area—between 9,400 and 9,800 feet—and transferring the distance between these two contours to the graphic scale. Using the metric side of the ruler gives 8 millimeters; you could have used the other edge and got 5⁄16 inch.

Slope Considerations

For those who are less mathematically inclined, the difference between percent grade and slope angle gets ugly. It invokes words like *sine*, *arctangent*, and *Pythagoras*.

Yet it's an important distinction. The gradient of your ascent, measured in the direction of travel, tells you how hard you'll be working. The slope angle, measured in the direction of gravity, tells you how dangerous a slope may be. A 38 percent grade is safe, but a 38 percent angle can kill—it's the prime angle for a slab avalanche.

Table 4.1 Two ways to describe the same hill

Slope angle	Percent grade
10°	19%
20°	37%
30°	58%
35°	70%
40°	84%
45°	100%
50°	120%
60°	178%
70°	275%

If you are a backcountry skier, snowboarder, or snowshoer, slope information becomes vital as it's the single most important factor in predicting avalanches. The highest probability of avalanche occurs on slope angles between 30° and 45°. Knowing this, you can plan a safe route that avoids significant hazards.

It's easy to calculate percent grade (rise over run) but harder to figure the angle from a map. For the moderate slopes on which you are likely to be hiking or skiing, simply divide the percent grade by two to get a rough approximation of slope angle. As Table 4.1 shows, this calculation is reasonably close for slopes up to 45°.

Winter travelers should memorize the critical grade range, which is 58 to 100 percent, with 70 to 84 percent really setting off the warning bells.

To simplify measuring slope angles on a topo, use a template similar to that shown in Figure 4.5.

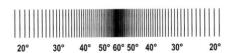

Figure 4.5 This slope gauge on the back of the Life-Link Slope Meter allows estimating angles directly from a 1:24,000 map.

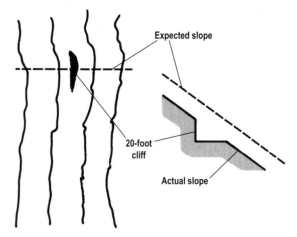

Figure 4.6 Hidden cliff.

These slope templates work by matching up the lines with the contour lines on the map. Be sure the template is at a right angle to the contours and carefully slide it back and forth until you get the closest match, then read the angle. Different scales require different templates, so be sure you are using the correct one for your map.

Warning: However carefully you measure on the map, calculate average gradients, and so on, you could be in for a nasty surprise. Theoretically, at least, a cliff less than 40 feet high could hide between 40-foot contours, just as a waterfall could account for most of the drop on a white-water river (see Figure 4.6).

5.

Direction from the Map

You already know the two crucial facts about directions and maps:

1. The maps we use show points in the landscape in the proper direction. A road that takes off at right angles from another appears on the map the same way.
2. The maps we use are oriented so that North is at the top.

Caveat: there are charts of entire oceans and maps of the world on which, due to the way a sphere is represented on paper, angles are inaccurate. On the small areas of our topographic maps, however, the first rule is universally true.

If North is at the top, East is to the right, South at the bottom, and West to the left. These four *cardinal points*—that is, principal points—are a good start for memorizing directions.

To describe a wind direction or some other direction—such as the trend of a river or trail—you go one step further to the *intercardinal* points, halfway between the cardinals, abbreviated NE, SE, SW, and NW. Few people will care to go to the three-letter directions, such as NNE between NE and N, or ENE between NE and E.

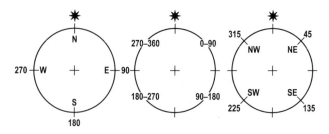

Figure 5.1 Compass degrees.

For precise directions, degrees numbered from 0° for North and running clockwise to back to 360° at North are much simpler.

Directions in Degrees

It is important to learn a few key directions expressed in degrees. That'll keep you from making gross errors, such as marching off in exactly the opposite direction.

There are two methods to help you with that. The first is based on nothing more complicated than learning the figures that correspond to the four cardinal points: 0° (or 360°) for North, 90° for East, 180° for South, and 270° for West.

You can readily see from Figure 5.1 that any direction between North and East must be in the range of numbers from 0° to 90°, between East and South in the range of 90° to 180°, and so on.

Since most mistakes are errors of 180° or, more rarely, of 90° or 270°, these four figures for the cardinals will catch most mistakes.

You can refine that system if you care to memorize the degrees that correspond to the intercardinals as well: NE corresponds to 45°, SE to 135°, SW to 225°, and NW to 315°.

Many people find another system more to their liking. It's based on the familiar twelve-hour clock face. Multiply the hour by thirty and you'll get the corresponding degrees. For example, multiply three o'clock

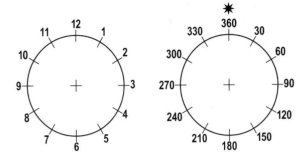

Figure 5.2 Clock face and compass degrees.

by thirty to get 90° (East), nine o'clock to get 270° (West), and so on (see Figure 5.2).

With this system, you can check the approximate direction from Milner Pass to the following points:

Unnamed twin peak, 11,961 feet
Unnamed twin peak, 11,881 feet
Shipler Mountain
Peak west of Lake Irene, 11,209 feet

Just imagine the clock face centered on the pass. The first peak is a bit past three o'clock; therefore, the direction is a little more than 90°. The measured directions are, in order, about 95°, 143°, 292°, and 240°.

Measuring Directions on Maps

Sailors have it easy. Their charts (that's nautical for maps) have compass roses, marked in degrees, printed at convenient places on the chart. To transfer lines from or to a compass rose, for measuring or plotting directions, marine navigators use parallel rules, two triangles, or drafting machines. But our maps have no compass roses.

Marine charts also have meridians and parallels of latitude printed on them. That allows you to use many kinds of protractors—long rectangular ones, square ones (large and small), and movable ones with or without arms.

Our maps have ticks in the margins and crosses in the map area itself where meridians and parallels of latitude cross. And, unless you have drawn in a UTM grid, that's it.

Though protractors are convenient for measuring direction, you can get along fine without one. Modern compasses—the type with a rectangular, transparent base and a compass needle in a housing that you can turn—serve as protractors.

Here is a standard problem: in what direction is point B from point A? Or less frighteningly put: in what direction should I move to get from where I am (on the map) to where I want to be? A navigator might call it the *course*.

There's another common problem: what mountain, lake, village, or whatever is it that I see over there?

You can get an estimate of the direction of the object you want to identify with any compass. With some compasses you can measure the direction quite accurately. A navigator would call it a *bearing* or, if he is given to fancier words, an *azimuth*.

You can see that this is very closely related to the course-finding problem. The question is: what mountain, lake, village, or whatever would I reach if I walked straight on that course?

Here's how modern compasses act as protractors, say, in finding a course.

Place either of the two long edges of the compass on the map to connect the two points of the problem. Call them *A* and *B*, or *start* and *destination*. The arrow on the baseplate, called the *direction-of-travel arrow*, must point to your destination.

Ignore the compass needle, but turn its enclosing capsule so the *N* mark points upward and the parallel lines are parallel with the left or right margin of the map. (Instead of the *N* mark, your compass may have two parallel lines forming a gate for the North-pointing end of the magnetic needle, or some other device, such

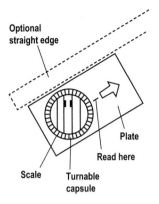

Figure 5.3 A baseplate compass acts as a protractor.

as two dots that glow in the dark to frame the luminous end of the needle.)

You can now read your course on the 360° scale at the bottom of the travel arrow.

If your map lacks a grid, perhaps you can't see how to align the lines of a compass capsule with the margins accurately when the compass is somewhere in the middle of the map.

There is a method. It is shown in Figure 5.3 and uses a ruler or straight edge as an aid to navigation:

1. Place the ruler on the map between A and B with one end of the ruler reaching the left or right margin of the map.
2. Place the compass alongside the ruler with one of its long edges touching the ruler and the direction-of-travel arrow pointing toward the destination, B.
3. Slide the compass along the ruler to the margin and turn the capsule, North mark up, until one of the parallel lines is parallel with the map margin.
4. You can now read the course on the degree scale at the base of the travel arrow.

Some people hate any sort of mathematics and may wonder if there is a way to do compass work without any figuring.

Direction from the Map   77

Good news: yes, there is. In fact, there are several.

First, there is the common use of compasses, especially by beginners. You use it only for such mundane purposes as deciding which fork in the road to take, or which of two trails. But you'd hardly call that navigation.

Then there is the situation in which you walk toward a visible landmark. Although you would not need a compass if you were able to keep your goal in sight at all times, the compass will keep you walking on a straight line even if you lose sight of it behind trees or hills.

In a narrow strip that now runs roughly from Superior, Wisconsin, through Illinois, to Biloxi, Mississippi, and in a few other areas of the world, you could work the course problem by simply following the magnetic needle's direction. In a similar way, you could lay your compass on the map to decide what landmark you were looking at without any figure work. You'll read about these techniques in Chapter 7, "Using Your Compass."

But most likely you will not always be in one of these strips that make compass work so easy. Elsewhere, as you probably remember, the compass needle points a bit west or east of true North. You must correct for that error.

The cheapest solution that takes little work is to apply the correction by adding it to or subtracting it from the course shown by the compass. You'd apply it to bearings by the opposite operation—subtracting or adding the correction. That can't be done without math.

But there are three ways out. One is to buy a compass that, once set for the error (which ashore is called *declination*, and at sea, *variation*), eliminates the mathematics from courses and bearings.

A second solution involving paper maps takes more work. After you find out what the local declination is, you draw a lot of parallel lines at that angle. Then you use these lines to set your compass capsule instead of aligning it with the map margins. If you've already drawn in a UTM grid, making these magnetic lines a different color can help but it's likely more information than you want.

A third option is to print custom digital maps that are oriented with magnetic North instead of true North. Be sure that everyone who uses them knows they are nonstandard, or they may use a corrected compass and end up off course.

For now, simply remember this: (1) some compasses can act as protractors, and (2) almost nowhere does the compass needle point toward true North.

Position Lines

The unifying concept in navigation is the notion of *lines of position*. Simply put, a position line is a line (in nature or on the map) on or near which you are at the moment, without knowing how far along the line you are.

Suppose you get on a Fifth Avenue bus. As you bump along you are certain you are on that avenue. But, being a stranger in town, you don't know just where on Fifth Avenue you are at any given time. A typical position line situation.

Then you see a street sign: 42nd Street. Your doubts are dissolved. You can think of that street as another position line.

You are on both these position lines at once, so you must also be at the point on the map where the two cross. In nautical language, which in this case is worth adopting for our use, you have a *fix*.

That is land navigation, but hardly what you had in mind when you opened this book. All right, here's an example closer to our subject. You are hiking a well-established, mapped trail. You have been going for some time. You are sure you're on the right trail, but how far have you come?

Now you cross a stream, clearly shown on the map. There is no other stream crossing within many miles.

Again, you are on two position lines at the same time, one the trail and the other the stream. Your position is pinpointed: you have a fix.

A power line, a cross trail, a fork in the trail, a saddle, the point where you enter or leave a national forest or a wilderness area (according to a trail sign)—these and many other landmarks would do as well to fix your position.

Another example: you walk a compass course in open terrain. You are sure of your direction, but the distance covered gets more doubtful with every hour you walk. Say the formula you use estimates distance accurately within ½ mile per hour; after three hours, the possible error is 1½ miles. You could be that distance ahead of or behind your calculated distance. An uncertainty of 3 miles (5 kilometers).

A marine navigator would call a similar position derived from course, speed, and time his *dead reckoning* position (a term supposedly derived from "deduced reckoning").

Now you notice two peaks on your right, one near, one more distant, coming almost into one line. You keep going until they exactly line up. Draw a straight line through the two peaks on the map and across your track. Again, being on two position lines at once, you are at their crossing point on the map.

Or near it, at least. However careful, you probably did not follow the compass course exactly. What seems to be the peak may be a point near it.

There are not enough such "transits" of two objects to navigate by. But with some compasses you can take bearings accurately enough to get good position lines.

On a mapped trail, one such bearing gives you a fix. (You may take a second bearing on another object as a check.) Off trail, or when you don't know which trail you're on, the intersection of two bearings can pinpoint your position.

Obviously the two bearings must be at different angles from you. Two objects in the same direction (angle 0°) or exactly opposite each other (angle 180°) are no better than a single bearing. The ideal lies halfway between these extremes. Try for bearings that differ by 90°. Usually you won't find two objects lined up just so, and you must settle for any angle between 45° and 135°–that is, 90° plus or minus 45°.

The accuracy of your bearing readings will determine the precision of your fix. If you aren't careful, it's easy to be off by 3° when taking the reading. And you might impose another 2° of error when plotting the bearing on a map, particularly with a small compass. This combined error of 5° translates to about 460 feet for every mile (90 meters per kilometer). If you take the reading off a peak 10 miles away, you could be off by nearly a mile. Slowing down and using a better compass (see Chapter 6) can greatly improve your fix.

Adding a third bearing allows you to triangulate your position. When the three bearings are drawn on the map, they almost never intersect at one spot. Instead, they create a triangle, which navigators call a "cocked hat," that contains your position roughly in the center.

Contour lines in combination with a small precision instrument that tells your present elevation, an *altimeter,* open up more position lines.

The trail you're on could be one position line, the contour line corresponding to your elevation the other. Usually, they cross only once; if they cross more often, your fix should be the one where they cross for the first time.

You don't even need a trail. Say you are hiking cross-country. Your elevation gives one position line; the other can come from a creek, a mapped fence, or the bearing of a peak you recognize.

You'll read more about these techniques in Chapter 9, "Altimeter Navigation." You'll even learn a method that gives your position on the map using only an accurate altimeter reading and nothing else–no trails, creeks, fences, or any visible landmarks.

Converging Map Margins

Some sharp-eyed readers will have noticed that the margins of the map of Colorado in Figure 3.1 converge. So, of course, do all the meridians on a globe.

You may have wondered whether the margins on 7½′ topographic maps converge. Yes, they do—a little.

If you align the south edge of the 7½′ quad from which our map was taken with that map's north edge, you'll find it ⅟₃₂ inch (¾ millimeter) longer. On the Rocky Mountain National Park map, on the same scale as the old 15′ quads but taking in almost twice as much latitude and longitude, the difference between north and south margins is about ⁵⁄₃₂ inch (4 millimeters).

Strictly speaking, we should align our compass with the left margin when the angle measured is near the left margin, and with the right margin when it's near the right. But the error caused by the convergence of the meridians in these small areas is less than the accuracy you expect or need. (The angle between one of the side margins and a vertical line through the center of the Rocky Mountain National Park is on the order of ⅛°.)

Similarly, the vertical lines on the UTM grid point true North only at the meridian of each zone (^{5}00^{000}E). Look at the declination arrows near the lower left corner of the map. One is labeled *MN* for magnetic North; the other is labeled *GN* for grid North. In the vast majority of cases, grid North is within a second of true North—not enough to worry about.

The compasses used for land navigation typically are calibrated at 2° intervals. But that brings us to Chapter 6, where you'll meet a representative collection of these protractor compasses.

6.

Choosing a Compass

This chapter is about compasses, especially the kind suitable for most outdoor activities.

Any compass, right down to the gumball machine model, lets you turn the map so that it approximately matches what you see in the field. It also lets you decide which branch of a trail leads east, which south. Other compasses let you do a lot more.

For our purposes, the choice is between the many compasses that act as their own protractors, to which you were introduced in Chapter 5. They are best suited to hikers, climbers, skiers, fishermen, hunters, and other recreational users.

And with good reason: these compasses are more versatile, faster, and handier—once you have learned to use them—than any other kind. You could call them "protractor compasses." However, most people refer to them as "baseplate compasses," since the baseplate is one of their chief advantages.

The best use for other types of compasses—zipper pull, pin-on, or wristwatch—is for cross-country skiers or trail runners who'd rather glance at a pin-on or wristwatch than take off gloves and unzip pockets. As a backup in case you lose your primary compass, they are better than nothing, barely.

Some GPS units have built-in electronic compasses that indicate direction when you are standing still or walking slowly (a standard GPS will not show direction unless it's moving; more on this later). However, these must be recalibrated every time the batteries are changed (a frequent event). And, since they have no transparent baseplate with a straight edge, they are not as useful for map work.

Remember: no matter how fancy the GPS unit, you still should have a backup compass when traveling in remote terrain.

All members of the party—except small children—should have their own compass. If you, Mr. Tour-guide, lose yours, you can always commandeer one.

Basic Types of Baseplate Compasses

The choice of baseplate compasses can be bewildering. Between the three major brands—Brunton, Silva, and Suunto—there are over forty models. To confuse matters further, Brunton compasses are labeled Silva outside of North America and have no relation to the Silva compasses sold here.

You can make the task of selecting a compass much easier—for the moment, at least—by disregarding minor conveniences: rubber feet to keep the compass from sliding off the map or built-in magnifiers. At this stage, disregard even the minor differences in size and weight.

Compasses come with a number of scales on as many as three edges. Inches (divided into eighths or tenths) and centimeters (divided into millimeters) are common. You'll find a metric version handy if you travel outside the United States.

Some compasses have a 1:25,000 scale, which is close enough to 1:24,000 USGS topos for most purposes. Others may have a 1:62,500 scale, which again works quite well on 1:63,360-scale maps.

A few compasses are designed to complement a GPS unit. In addition to providing reliable backup, these have UTM roamer scales on the baseplate that correspond to common map scales. If your maps have UTM grids, a compass with roamer scales greatly simplifies the task of reading coordinates.

Even the divisions of the degree scale, which allow you to use the compass as a protractor, don't matter terribly much. Some compasses are graduated in 5° intervals, but most of them are in 2° steps.

The only magnetic compasses to consider have jeweled bearings and are liquid damped to bring the needle to rest quickly. The needles in handheld air-filled models never really stop their jitters, and you may have water seepage troubles. They also need a needle-lifter mechanism to save wear on the needle bearing.

The liquid in these compasses freezes at about −40°F. An occasional *small* air bubble in the liquid does not affect the performance of the compass. If you get a large bubble, return the compass. If the liquid can't get out, water can't get in, either.

The bottom of the capsule that houses the compass needle is transparent. That lets you align the capsule with map margins or whatever, as briefly discussed in Chapter 5 and in detail in the next few chapters.

The North end of the needle is clearly marked, though not necessarily with the letter N. More often, you match the shape and color of the end of the needle with a corresponding design in the capsule. That makes the identification of the correct end of the needle just about idiot-proof.

All but the cheapest models have luminous points that help in night work; some dials are even luminescent. Unless you have a light of your own, you should probably not be walking around in the dark anyway. A luminous compass will not prevent you from turning an ankle.

The prices (as of 2005) are for guidance only. Even though they are likely to change, they give an indication of how much each step up in features may add.

Now to the major decisions. There are two you need to make.

First, will you be satisfied with taking bearings by merely pointing the baseplate of the compass at the target? That should get you within 4°, for a total error of probably not more than 8°.

For identifying a feature in the landscape, that's probably good enough. (An error of 4° to either side is about the distance on the horizon covered by four of your fingers, arm outstretched.)

Over a distance of 1 mile, a 4° error amounts to being 380 feet off to one side or the other. Over 3 miles, that makes an error on the order of 1,200 feet. (In metric units: over a distance of 1 kilometer, a 4° error amounts to about 70 meters off to one side or the other. Over 5 kilometers, that makes an error on the order of 350 meters.)

For fixing your position accurately, such bearings are poor—and the farther the target of your bearing, the worse it gets. We'll cover that in more detail later.

If your answer is "Yes, it's good enough," pick a basic compass without a mirror (see Figures 6.1, 6.2, 6.3, 6.4). If not, choose a model with either direct sighting (see Figure 6.7) or a mirror (see Figures 6.5, 6.6, 6.8).

Second, are you willing to correct for declination for every course and every bearing by calculation or by drawing lines on your maps?

If yes, then there are several basic options available and a few specialized models available (see Figures 6.1, 6.7).

If, on the other hand, you want to set your compass for the declination in the region and then mostly forget about it, choose a model with declination adjustment built in. Considering the minimal price increase, these are the best choice for most people (see Figures 6.2, 6.3, 6.4. 6.5, 6.6, 6.8)

This feature allows the option of using bearings for fixing position, and reading bearings and courses directly from the compass. Although the work of calculating declinations can be tedious, the bigger concern is the possibility of making an error in a stressful situation. For instance, when you're tired and wet, you add when you should be subtracting. (And it's easy to get confused—in one part of the country you add to courses and subtract from bearings; in another part, you subtract from courses and add to bearings.)

Figure 6.1 The Brunton 7DNL (0.8 ounce, $11) is a good-quality, no-frills compass. It has a declination scale, but you must do the math.

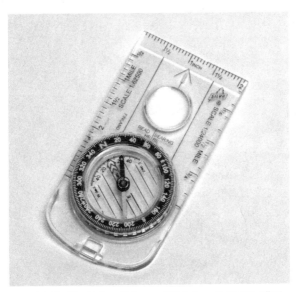

Figure 6.2 The Silva Explorer (1.0 ounce, $23) features declination adjustment, scales for USGS maps, and a magnifier.

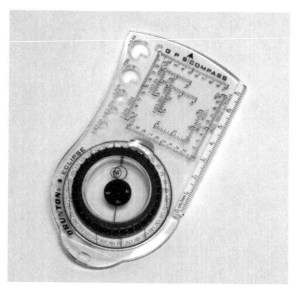

Figure 6.3 Brunton 8096 GPS (1.7 ounces, $40) features UTM roamer scales and 100-meter confidence circles for five different map scales. It also has a ruler that flips for inches or millimeters.

Figure 6.4 The Silva Cobalt (2.1 ounces, $60) is a digital compass with a baseplate that can take bearings off of a map. It has a timer and alarms to warn you when you deviate from the route.

Choosing a Compass

Figure 6.5 The Suunto MC-2G (2.7 ounces, $55) has a unique gimbal-mounted needle that allows it to be used anywhere on the planet—a good choice for visits to the other hemisphere.

Figure 6.6 Silva Ranger Ultra 530 (2.6 ounces, $68) is an improvement on the classic Ranger. It adds a sighting slot in the mirror for more accurate readings, a 1:25,000 UTM roamer scale, and a magnifying glass.

Choosing a Compass

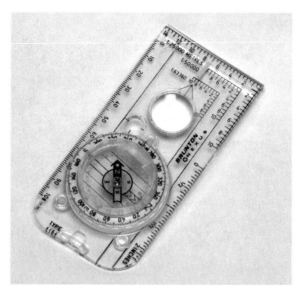

Figure 6.7 The Brunton 54LU (1.4 ounces, $78) has a unique direct sighting system that is very accurate (±½-degree accuracy) and provides a back bearing. But there is no magnetic declination adjustment or scale.

Figure 6.8 The Brunton 8099 Pro (3.9 ounces, $99) offers three ways to measure slope angles and provides an abundance of other features. It is particularly suited to forestry applications.

Choosing a Compass

If you make a mistake, the consequences can be serious. Say the declination is 15°. If you do the figuring wrong, you'll be 30° off. That's 3,000 feet over a distance of 1 mile (580 meters per kilometer).

The advantage of the set-and-forget system is that you don't have to work with numbers at all. You get courses off the map and walk them by compass, unconcerned about how many degrees from North the offset must be. Or you take a bearing and plot it on the map without ever having to read the degree scale.

Fine Points to Consider

After you've determined that a compass meets basic standards, you can narrow your search by considering the more sophisticated features.

Dip

You should buy your compass where it is to be used. This doesn't mean you can't use a compass in Montana that you bought in Idaho, or the other way round. But the compass that gave you good service in the United States will hang up in Australia, Argentina, Chile, and the southern part of Africa.

The earth's magnetic field not only dictates the direction of the compass needle but also makes it tilt from horizontal (toward North in the United States). This effect is known as *dip* or, if you must have a longer term, *magnetic inclination*.

Imagine a compass needle arranged not as in a compass, but instead free to take any position in a vertical plane. Only along a line known as the *magnetic equator* will the needle rest horizontally. This line gently curves around the geographic equator, staying roughly within 10°N and 15°S.

As you get farther from that line, the dip of the needle generally increases. In Australia it is between 40° and 70° toward the South. In the United States, southern Canada, and Europe it is 55° to 75° toward the North.

Compass makers overcome the tendency of the needle to dip by counterbalancing the needle, sometimes using nothing more complicated than a drop of paint. The world is divided into five zones (see Figure 6.9) and your compass should be fine one zone away, say in Central America, and part way into the second zone, such as Bolivia.

If you plan to backcountry travel in the southern latitudes, buy your compass there or order one for use in that area before you leave home. Some global models use a gimbal mount for the needle to allow use anywhere (see Figure 6.5).

Types of Scales

The compasses we are talking about come with a 360° scale as a rule, in the United States at least. But there are other scales. Some surveyors prefer a scale divided into four quadrants that run from 0° to 90°. Others insist on four hundred subdivisions, called *grads,* in place of the 360°. A right angle in that system is, of course, 100 grads. Making a 180° turn becomes making a 200-grad turn.

Worse yet are *mils.* They are optional alongside degree marks on some compasses, the only markings on others.

If you drew a circle with a 1,000-foot (or 1,000-meter) radius, it would have a circumference of about 6,283 feet (or 6,283 meters). That provides a basis for dividing the whole circle. The divisions are much finer than mere degrees, which appeals to the military. But dividing the circle into that odd number was just too much. So military planners divided it into 6,400 sectors instead and called them mils. (To confuse the enemy, some nations have adopted 6,000 divisions.)

The only place you'll encounter mils is in the declination diagram on topographic maps, where they are given alongside the same information in degrees. One degree equals about 18 mils.

The reason for mentioning all these strange scales is to prepare you for the questions of a salesperson and

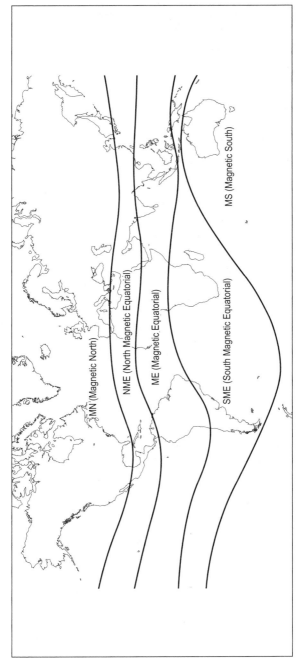

Figure 6.9 Magnetic inclination zones. A quality compass is calibrated for the zone in which it is sold. An MN compass works reasonably well in the NME zone. It still functions farther south by tilting the baseplate, but mirror sighting may not be possible. A global compass works anywhere.

to prevent disappointment when you open the parcel containing your mail-order compass the day before your departure for Chile. You should ask for clockwise 360° scales.

Compasses Designed for High Accuracy

When you shop for a compass, you may see much fancier models designed for professional use. Keep in mind that unless they have at least one straight edge corresponding to the long edges on a baseplate compass, they can't be used in the simple manner of the protractor compasses. This is also a major drawback of most digital compasses.

You may be tempted to get a compass that lets you take more accurate bearings than the mirror-sighting models permit. Lensatic (using lenses), prismatic (using prisms), and optical sighting compasses are used by the military and by timber cruisers and other professionals.

Unless such compasses are robust—which unfortunately often means heavy and expensive—their accuracy will prove an illusion.

The problem with most sighting compasses, however well made, is that they must be held level, so you cannot take sights of peaks from the valley, or of the valley from a peak. If you have to bring the peak down to your level mentally, you lose all of the accuracy for which you have paid.

Buying a Baseplate Compass

When you have decided on the compass model you want, need, or can afford at the moment, by all means spend some time on the purchase. Unless you lose it, which is not likely if you use its lanyard, the compass will be with you for decades.

However, if you don't live near a well-stocked mountain shop, don't hesitate to order a compass through the Internet. Any reputable mail-order dealer will exchange a compass that fails any of the tests described below. Most of them will also accept returns if you don't like the feel of a specific model.

Just as the heft of a hammer or the feel of a screwdriver makes the difference between a tool you feel comfortable with and a tool that merely drives nails or turns screws, so one compass will suit you better than another of perhaps equal quality and price.

Look especially at the 360° scales. Some are easier to read than others; a few even have magnifiers for the scale (see Figures 6.3, 6.8). Readability often has little to do with price.

Then look at the North end of the needle and the design you are to match it with. When navigating at night, a backlight (see Figure 6.4), luminous dial (see Figure 6.5), or at least bright needle and North markings (see Figures 6.6, 6.7) can help.

When you have made your decision, the salesperson is likely to hand you a brand-new compass. Check to make sure there are no bubbles in the liquid of the capsule. It should show North where other compasses do.

Next check how the capsule turns. If it hurts your fingers, get another specimen; perhaps a different model if the stiffness and sharp edges are family traits.

Next see if the capsule has excessive side play. Turn the compass until the needle is in the slot or whatever design that compass uses. Then try to move the capsule east and west. If the reading at the index mark changes by more than 1°, try another compass.

If the compass has index marks both near and away from you, make sure they are in line. When one reads 180° the other should read 360° or 0°, not 358° or 2°.

Mirror Sight

A mirror sight increases the accuracy of bearings by allowing you to view distant objects and the compass dial without moving your head.

Hold the compass horizontally in front of you and make sure that you can sight on an object near the ceiling (compass somewhat above eye level) and then on the floor a few feet away (compass somewhat below eye level) while watching the needle in the mirror. Some models have a cutout at the base of the mirror that aids downward sighting.

In addition to greatly improving accuracy, a compass mirror is useful for changing contact lenses or shaving beards. And on sunny days it can be used for signaling in an emergency.

Declination Adjustment

Have the salesperson show you how the declination adjustment works. Or ask to be left alone with the instruction book, which should be fairly clear on that subject.

Some compasses are adjusted with a small screwdriver blade threaded on the lanyard. Adjust others with your bare fingers by turning the inner capsule; since there is no metal, these hold up better around salt water.

You won't have to adjust it very often. In the area of our map, for example, you'd readjust it after you had traveled 100 miles (160 kilometers) east or west, and after a much greater distance if you traveled north or south.

Clinometer

Some models can be used to measure the angle of a slope (see Figures 6.5, 6.6, 6.8). This is valuable information for backcountry skiers and snowshoers who need to avoid avalanche terrain. Most avalanches occur on slopes between 30° and 45°. But these slope angles are actually tricky to spot and most people guess wrong.

Test the baseplate clinometer by turning the capsule until the inner scale lines up with North and South. Hold the compass on its side and read the angle from the pendulum needle; this should be a fast, simple procedure. It sometimes helps to lay a ski pole on the snow and then hold the compass against it.

Foresters use clinometers to determine the heights of trees. But this requires a more accurate angle mea-

Figure 6.10 The Brunton Clino Master (4.0 ounces, $136) quickly reads angles with 1/2-degree accuracy.

surement, which involves a fancier sighting system (see Figure 6.8) or a specialized instrument (see Figure 6.10). Clinometers come with tangent tables so you just multiply the angle's tangent by the distance from the base to get the height.

Marine Compasses

For sea kayaking, or even canoeing on large lakes, a deck-mounted marine compass is a useful navigation aid. This saves putting the paddle down to use a hand-held compass, so you can easily maintain a heading. And you can get a bearing just by pointing your boat at an object.

Most marine compasses suitable for a sea kayak are direct reading, which means the heading is taken from the front of the capsule nearest your eye. The gradations are of either 5° or 10°, which is sufficient for the job. Some also give a reciprocal bearing so you don't have to do any math.

Automobile Compasses

Sometimes the hardest navigation is to the trailhead by back roads, where a forest map and a compass would help. You may not feel like getting out of your car and walking 30 feet (10 meters) away from it so your hiking compass can do some undisturbed navigation.

There are compasses specially made for automobiles. They are not terribly accurate—every steel part in an automobile attracts the magnetic element in the compass, and every direct current throws it off—but they are useful when properly placed and adjusted.

An automobile compass, even a fancy digital model, won't work right if you just take it out of its box and mount it any place. Read the instructions on where to place the compass and how to adjust it—that is, how to compensate for the car's magnetic fields, both mechanical and electrical. It usually works something like this:

Step 1. Put the car on a heading of magnetic East. With a nonmagnetic screwdriver (a dime, or a blade whittled from a piece of hardwood), make the compass read East by turning the screw marked (usually) *E-W*. If nothing happens, you are turning the wrong adjusting screw. If the compass reading moves away from East instead of toward it, you're turning the right screw the wrong way.

Step 2. Put the car on a heading of magnetic North. By turning the other screw, marked (usually) *N-S*, make the compass read North. If nothing happens, you are turning the wrong screw and have just canceled the first adjustment. Start over. If the compass reading moves away from North instead of toward it, you are turning the correct screw the wrong way.

Step 3. Put the car on a magnetic heading of West. With the first screw you used, remove one-half of the remaining error. If, for example, the compass indicates 10° from West, turn the East-West screw until the error is only 5°.

Step 4. Put the car on a magnetic heading of South. Using the second screw, marked *N-S*, again remove half of the remaining error. And that's about the best you can do.

Make sure there are no overhead power lines nearby that may influence your compass when you are adjusting it. Find the cardinal headings with your hiking compass with the car a good distance off so it won't throw off your hiking compass.

Don't expect a perfect adjustment. Check what various circuits in the car do to your adjustment. If you find, for example, that turning on the electric windshield wipers upsets your careful adjustment, trust your compass only when the wipers are off.

Don't expect too much accuracy from any car compass and don't forget that if you move it, even only a hand's width, you have to readjust it.

When in doubt, walk away from your vehicle and use your baseplate compass where it is not disturbed by automotive parts and electrical circuits (including those in transistor radios, exposure meters, and so on).

Unless you need the extra features (such as an altimeter or thermometer), there is no advantage to spending a lot more for an automobile compass. Even the best will not be very accurate once you install it in your vehicle. But it'll keep you from starting out in the wrong direction or taking the wrong fork—and so will a well-adjusted, less-expensive compass.

Compass Care

If you treat a quality compass with respect, it will probably outlive you. On the other hand, if you pretend it's indestructible, you could be in for a rude awakening.

The big no-no with any compass is strong magnetic fields, which can actually reverse the polarity—the needle points to South instead of North. Or the needle may be partially reversed, evidenced by slow or confused response.

This can happen due to exposure to a magnet, such as in a stereo speaker. Also, rapid movement of the compass within a few inches of an electrical current can mess with things. And even storing a compass next to large steel objects can affect polarity. Note that the antennas in avalanche transceivers, radios, and cell phones are made with magnets, so don't store your compass near them.

If you suspect a compass has been partially or fully reversed, first compare it to one that is known to work properly. If your compass is indeed off, it's possible to re-polarize it by stroking the North (red) end of the needle outward from the South end of a strong magnet. Check the results against another compass.

A more common problem is the formation of an air bubble in the liquid capsule of the compass. As you increase in altitude, the air bubble gets larger and can interfere with the needle movement.

In general, small bubbles (diameter of a pencil eraser or less) are considered normal and do not affect performance; they will disappear when you return to lower altitudes. However, larger bubbles indicate a hairline crack in the capsule from a hard shock. If the compass is fairly new, it may be replaced under warranty. But if you've had it for a couple of years, consider it a lesson in taking better care of equipment, and purchase a new compass.

Also take care to avoid letting it come into contact with any solvents, including insect repellant. These will attack the acrylic and cause it to turn milky white so you can no longer see through the baseplate. Solvents can also remove the markings on the compass dial.

7.

Using Your Compass

In this chapter, to simplify things, let's assume we are in an area of virtually no declination or are using a set-and-forget model already set for the local declination. How to find and live with declination is the subject of Chapter 8.

All makes and models of baseplate compasses are handled in the same manner. It's somewhat like driving a car. If you know how to drive a Chevrolet, you can also drive a Ford.

The only difference in compasses is in how you take a bearing: by looking at a mirror on some models; by just pointing the compass in others. It's comparable to the difference between a stick shift and an automatic transmission.

Leaving out such goodies as lanyards, magnifiers, slope-measuring devices, and map scales, baseplate compasses are fairly simple devices (see Figure 7.1). Like other analog compasses, they have a magnetized needle that turns on a jeweled bearing on a pivot. The entire assembly is enclosed in a capsule that you can turn with respect to the baseplate. Both the plate and the capsule are transparent to let you see the map underneath them.

A degree dial (azimuth ring) read against a stationary mark indicates how far you have turned the capsule. The mark is typically at the base of an arrow that indicates the direction of travel or of sighting.

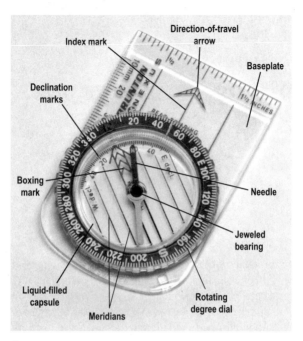

Figure 7.1 Parts of a baseplate compass.

On folding mirror models, the mirror is hinged where the arrow ought to start. A line (often luminous) acts as an index mark, and the mirror itself indicates the direction of travel. On some compasses, you'll find a second index mark, perhaps also luminous, exactly opposite the main one.

A design corresponding to the end of the compass needle that points toward North is drawn on the top or bottom of the capsule. The details vary. It may be an arrow, a gate formed by two bars, or a circle. This *boxing mark* is often color coded to correspond with the red end of the needle. If the needle is luminous, the arrow or gate design will also glow in the dark.

The term that describes the activity of putting the North end of the compass needle over the boxing mark is *box the needle*. This has a nice nautical ring, reminiscent of "boxing the compass," used to describe the recital of the thirty-two compass directions by points

(11¼° increments) in proper clockwise order; this was once a basic skill mastered by all sailors. Some compasses use a circle-within-a-circle to orient the capsule toward North, but the principle is the same.

You'll box the needle a lot in this chapter and in using your compass. You can see that you can get the North end of the needle into its box in two ways. Either you turn the whole compass, or you turn only the capsule.

Sometimes you use one method and sometimes the other. It sounds confusing, but there is a very logical way to remember which method to use:

> If you have just set the capsule—in order to get a course off the map, for example—you turn the entire compass.

> If you have just turned the whole compass—in order to get the bearing of a peak, for example—you turn the capsule.

Parallel to the boxing mark on the top or bottom of the capsule, you'll usually find a set of lines. They are variously called *orienting lines, meridians,* or *North-South lines.*

You'll recall that meridians in geography are the lines that run from pole to pole on a map or a globe. You'll often be aligning the lines in the capsule with the meridians on your map.

Unless you've drawn in declination or UTM grid lines, you'll likely have only two meridians on topo maps: the left and the right margin of the quad. Often it's good enough to align the lines in the capsule with the margins of the map by the eyeball method, perhaps assisted by creases from folding. The UTM grid is best when greater accuracy is needed since you don't need a ruler or straightedge.

Since North on maps is at the top, the mark that indicates North in the capsule must be at the top when you align the capsule meridians with the map meridians; this is called *aligning the meridians.*

Preliminary Practice

Put your compass on a table and slowly rotate it. You'll discover that as you turn the baseplate in any direction the needle stays still.

Around the house, you'll make another discovery: The direction of the needle changes depending on what you set down near the compass. A knife, a paper clip, or anything made of steel, not to mention electric circuits such as those in cell phones, avalanche transceivers, and GPS units, will deflect the needle. Moral: keep such items away from your compass. Metal belt buckles, even when they look like brass, are also suspect. The error caused by such influences on the compass needle is called *deviation*.

Next, if you have not yet tried it, practice boxing the needle by both turning the capsule and turning the baseplate.

If you have a topo quad, put the compass down anywhere on it and align the meridians by eye only. If there are red survey lines on the map, you can use them as a guide.

If you don't have a map handy, use a newspaper. Pretend the left margin of the first column and the right margin of the last one are map margins.

First, place the compass in three different positions at random, the direction-of-travel arrow pointing every which way, and align the meridians. Remember that the boxing mark is always at the top.

For the next practice you'll need a ruler or similar straightedge. Again, place the compass randomly and align the meridians by eye alone. But now go one step further. Slide the compass along one edge of the ruler toward the right or left map or column margin (see Figure 7.2).

Are the lines in the capsule exactly aligned? If they are, you have a better feel for the vertical than most people, or else you have just been lucky.

To eliminate the luck hypothesis, try this test a few more times with the baseplate pointing nearly up or down and nearly left or right.

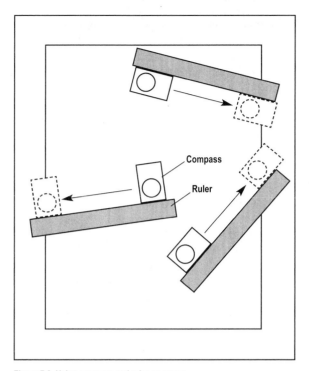

Figure 7.2 Using compass and ruler on a map.

After a few tries, aligning the meridians becomes an almost automatic routine. And you won't forget to have the box on top.

Serious Compass Work

We are now ready to practice map-and-compass work.

Normally we work with map and compass together. But the first technique of compass work described below needs no map.

Walking a Field Bearing

This involves using your compass to get the direction of your destination, then following the compass to get there.

Perhaps that does not make sense to you. Why would you need a compass to reach something in plain sight?

An example: you are standing on Milner Pass and want to climb one of the twin peaks, the one 11,881 feet high on our map that lies on the Continental Divide. For some reason you want to do so by the most direct route. You may regret that choice of route; it climbs 1,123 feet in $7/10$ mile (340 meters in $1\frac{1}{10}$ kilometers). Not having a map, you don't know that. But you can plainly see that after just a few minutes you'll be in the woods and probably lose sight of the peak. (We know this because of the green tint on the map.) To find your way to that peak, or any other destination you may lose sight of during the journey, proceed as follows:

Step 1. Aim the direction-of-travel arrow of your compass at your target. Face your destination squarely and hold the compass horizontally, in one hand (you'll need the other in the next step), and chest high.

When the target is higher than you are, it helps to look at the peak, then down toward the compass, and back up at the peak. If the target is lower than you are, say a lake seen from a peak, you may be able to look at it through the baseplate, which makes accurate aiming easy.

With a mirror sight you could, of course, just open the cover all the way until it is even with the baseplate and use it like a simple plate compass. But that's not using such a compass to full advantage.

A better method is to open the cover partway and aim it approximately at the target by looking at the V-sight with one eye. Adjust the cover so that you can see the capsule in the mirror (see Figure 7.13). That means holding the compass at about eye level; a little higher for a target higher than your location, somewhat lower for the target below you.

Step 2. Box the needle by turning the capsule with your right hand while aiming your compass at the target.

If you're using the mirror compass, the black line in the mirror must run through the center of the compass and the index mark (see Figure 7.14).

Step 3. Walk, snowshoe, ski, or whatever to your destination—without reading the degree scale at all—simply by keeping the needle boxed (see Figure 7.6).

It's awkward to walk with a compass in your hand, and nearly impossible to ski or snowshoe. So point your compass ahead, with the needle boxed, and look for a landmark such as a rock or a prominent tree. Then walk, ski, or snowshoe toward that landmark. When you get there repeat the process and find yourself another intermediate mark.

If using a mirror compass, look through your V-sight with the needle boxed and the black line in the mirror running through the center of the compass until you locate a landmark on the course to your target. Continue from landmark to landmark until you reach the destination.

Such intermediate marks serve us well. Suppose you come to a stream without a bridge. Find a mark on your line of position on the other side of the stream. Then go upstream or downstream until you find a bridge or ford. Once across the stream, just walk to your mark. When you reach it, resume your course as if you had never deviated from it.

The instruction "without reading the degree scale at all," used above, may bother some readers. Suppose you decide to give up on the steep climb and return to your car parked at Milner Pass. How can you make a 180° turn when you don't know what your original course was?

That's easy. Walk in the direction opposite to the one in which the direction-of-travel arrow points. The easiest way to do this is to box the South end of the needle rather than the North end for the return trip.

You'll be surprised how much of this problem—admittedly not a common one—pertains to other problems presented below.

Walking a Given Course

Suppose a friend invites you to use his cabin. He tells you exactly where to park your car. "And from there," he says, "you walk about 1 mile, 140° by compass. You won't see the cabin until you are almost there."

The problem is similar to the one presented in the section above; and again you don't need a map.

Step 1. Turn the capsule to set the course—140°—at the index mark. That'll be at the base of the direction-of-travel arrow on a simple compass, near the center of the mirror hinge on a mirror-sight model.

Step 2. With the compass in your hand, turn your whole body, feet included, to box the needle. If you didn't cheat by just twisting your hips or your wrist, your feet now face the destination.

With a mirror sight you can't cheat. Turn your body, again feet and all, until you have boxed the needle with the black line through the middle. What you see in the V of the sight is your first landmark.

Step 3. Walk, ski, or snowshoe in the direction you are facing, keeping the needle boxed. Or better yet, sight on landmarks, one after the other, until you reach the cabin.

A practical application of that technique might be found in guidebooks: "A spring is located ¼ mile distant, bearing 140° from the peak." People who don't know how to walk a given course go thirsty.

Orienting the Map

This is the simplest example of using map and compass together. It means positioning the map so that it matches what you see. Since maps have North at the top, you turn the map with the aid of a compass so that its top edge is facing North.

If your scenery and map include Half Dome, Mount Rushmore, or the Matterhorn, you simply turn the map by what you see. If any of these mountains are lined up with the map, everything on the map is lined up with the real world.

But what do you do when there are no recognizable features around, say in the Florida Everglades?

Step 1. Turn the capsule until 0° (360° or simply N on some models) is at the index mark, which you'll

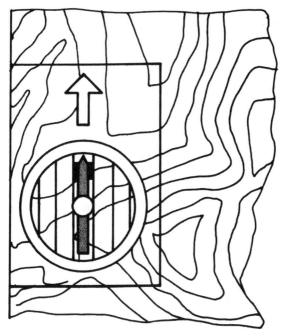

Figure 7.3 Orienting the map.

recall is at the base of the direction-of-travel arrow or at the middle of the hinge on the mirror-sight models.

Step 2. Place the compass with the travel arrow pointing toward the top of the map along the left or right margin of the map.

Step 3. Turn map and compass together until the needle is boxed. Now North on the map and North in the landscape are in the same direction. And so, of course, are all other directions. (See Figure 7.3.)

With baseplate compasses, orienting a map is seldom necessary. You most likely will use the technique to identify the peaks, lakes, and villages you see from some lookout point.

Your hiking map may not take in enough territory to identify distant features; you may need a map on a scale of about 1:250,000, which in the latitude covered by our map takes in about 70 by 110 statute miles (110 by 170 kilometers).

Finding a Course from the Map

This is probably the most often used map-and-compass operation. The steps are illustrated in Figures 7.4 through 7.9.

Step 1. Place one of the back corners of your compass on your starting position on the map. Turn the compass until the same edge is on your destination. If you start with a back corner, the direction-of-travel arrow automatically points in the right direction.

On a 1:24,000-scale map, this will work if the two points are no more than a mile or two apart. In the mountains, you can rarely walk even that far in a straight line. But in the desert your compass is just too short to reach a destination more than one hour's walk away. Even the open cover of a mirror-sight model doesn't make it long enough.

In this situation, you can lay a straightedge from start to destination, and then place the compass alongside, making sure the direction-of-travel arrow points toward the destination.

Step 2. Turn the capsule—with the boxing mark upward—to align its lines with the left or right margin of the map. Disregard the compass needle at this stage.

You can align the capsule by eye alone as you did in the preliminary practice at the beginning of this chapter, or with nearby survey lines. For greater accuracy, slide the compass along the straightedge to one of the vertical margins of the map and align the meridians with that. The first two course-finding operations require only a map and compass and could have been performed indoors. Now you have to step out into the landscape, or to use a shorter term, the *field.*

Step 3. With the compass in your hand, turn your body (feet and all) until the compass needle gets into the box. The direction-of-travel arrow, or the wide-open cover of a mirror compass, now points toward your destination.

For greater accuracy using a mirror-sight compass, box the needle (with the black line through the center of the needle and the index mark), and then look up through the V of the sight directly at your target.

Any prominent object in the sight, or in line with the direction-of-travel arrow on the simpler compasses, is your intermediate landmark.

Sometimes you get lucky: some distant object beyond your destination happens to be exactly in line with it. You may be aiming to reach a saddle with a peak behind it that happens to be in exactly the same direction. In these rare cases—which are often easily verified on the map, by laying your ruler from your position across the saddle to the peak, for example—you might as well put away your compass and walk toward the distant landmark using only your eyes.

Sailors call this imaginary line between two points a *transit*. When canoeing and sea kayaking, this is an invaluable technique for combating drift from currents and wind.

A small warning: it's tempting to use a star or a planet, which looks just like a star, as a distant landmark when walking at night, say in the desert to take advantage of the coolness. But the stars don't stand still. How fast they drift, and even in which direction in some parts of the sky, isn't easy to figure out. Best advice: enjoy your walk toward a star (or planet), but after ten minutes, check your compass. You may have to walk a bit to the left (or sometimes right) of your star. Check again after ten minutes. Eventually you'll find a new star to guide you.

Finding a Mapped Object

This problem is closely related to finding a course. When you know where you are, consider that as the starting point, the mapped object as the destination. Work out the course as described above.

When you have the needle boxed, you are looking straight at the feature you want to find—a peak, lake, saddle, or whatever. With the mirror-sight compass, you can actually put the object you want to find in your sight.

Identifying a Mapped Object

From a known position, you see an object so prominent you can assume it will be found on your topo map.

What looks like a small pond may be just the remains of the last snow to melt and will be gone in a week; it will not be mapped. But a good-sized lake is certain to be mapped.

Say you want to know what peak it is over there that you can see from the peak you're standing on.

In the last two problems, we asked, "What course must I walk, or in what direction must I aim the compass, to hit that destination or mapped object?" Here the question is, "If I walked (or aimed my compass) in that direction, what feature on the map would I reach?" Each step is illustrated in Figures 7.10 through 7.15.

Step 1. Start by taking a sight; that is, point the direction-of-travel arrow in a simple plate compass, or use V-sight and mirror as before.

Step 2. Turn the capsule to box the needle.

Step 3. Place one rear corner of your compass on your position on the map, and turn the entire compass—not the capsule—so that the lines in the capsule run parallel to the vertical map margins or UTM lines, as always with the boxing mark on top.

The edge of the compass you used for your position in the course-finding problem now points—in the direction-of-travel arrow—toward the object to be identified. If the compass is too short, use your ruler along that edge to make it longer.

When there is a possibility of confusion with a nearby similar object, say another peak close to the one you want to identify, use your ruler for aligning the compass from the map margin. Usually there's no worry and the extra accuracy is not needed.

For example, you and your party have just reached the point in section 12 of our map where the Red Mountain Trail meets the Grand Ditch. Your daughter asks, "What's the name of the mountain over there?"

You hand her your map and compass and instruct her as above.

When she puts the compass on the map and turns it to make the lines in the capsule parallel to the vertical edges of the map, there is no doubt: she was looking at Shipler Mountain. And you have another compass expert in your family.

The next problem is closely related to this one.

Getting a Position Line from a Known Object

Here we know where the mapped object is but don't know our position.

For example, where are you when, walking along the Grand Ditch, you measure the bearing of the more northerly summit of Shipler Mountain as 83°?

In the last example, it mattered little which peak your daughter sighted on. A simple plate compass was all that was needed. Even if she had been a couple of degrees off in setting the capsule lines parallel with the map margins, it wouldn't have mattered. She would still have got Shipler Mountain and no other for her answer.

But for getting your position from a bearing, the greater the accuracy, the closer to the real position you will be.

A compass with a mirror sight, properly handled, is highly recommended for this type of problem. And don't align the capsule by eye only; use the ruler and the map margin.

The technique for taking the bearing, also called the *azimuth*, is the same as before:

Step 1. Aim a simple baseplate compass, or get the target in the V-sight of a mirror model.

Step 2. Turn the capsule to box the needle.

Now the instructions have to differ. You don't know your position, so you can't place a rear corner of the compass on it. Instead, do this:

Step 3. Place a front corner of your compass on the known object on the map.

Step 4. Turn the entire compass—not the capsule—so that the lines in the capsule run parallel to the vertical map margin. (In this example you have a range line conveniently located right under your capsule.)

The edge of the compass you have used for getting a course is now along your position line. If the compass is too short to reach your position, use the ruler. You'll find you are near the bench mark 10,241.

Don't let the direction-of-travel arrow mislead you. As in the last problem, your position is near the rear of the compass on the map, just like the starting position when you are finding a course.

The *bearing* of Shipler Mountain here is the *course* a bird starting from your position would fly to reach the northerly peak.

You already know that you don't need a road or a trail to fix your position. You could have done that from two bearings. As you can guess, finding your position from two bearings is the mainstay of navigation in cross-country travel.

Summary

In this chapter, you were shown how walking a field bearing or a given course, finding a course from the map, finding or identifying a mapped object, and getting a position line from a bearing are all variations of the same basic operations. Other books skip many of these routines or present each as a separate routine to be memorized. However, you will understand them better if you can see how they are related.

Simply remember:

On the *map* you always work with the *lines* of the capsule.

In the *field* you always work with the compass *needle*.

The following illustrations will help you visualize the most important routines. The drawings and captions can also serve as a quick review when you have gone hazy between trips.

Basic Procedure for Finding a Course

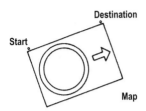

Figure 7.4 Lay a rear corner of the compass on your starting point on the map, one long edge pointing to your destination. Ignore capsule and needle. Double-check: arrow must point toward destination.

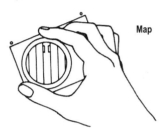

Figure 7.5 Hold the compass in place on the map. Turn the capsule until the gate is up and lines are parallel with left or right map margin. Ignore needle. Double-check: gate must be up.

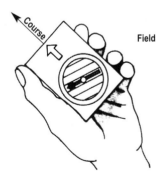

Figure 7.6 Holding the compass in front of you, turn your entire body until the needle is boxed in the gate. You and the arrow now face your destination. Double-check: the needle's North end must be in the gate.

More Accurate Procedure for Finding a Course

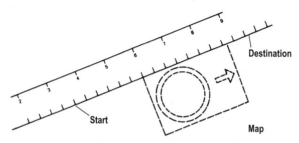

Figure 7.7 Align a ruler between the starting point and the destination. Lay the compass with one long edge alongside the ruler with the arrow pointing toward the destination. Ignore the capsule and needle. Double-check: the arrow must point toward the destination.

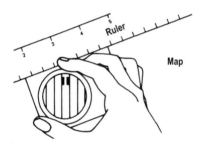

Figure 7.8 Holding the ruler and compass steady, turn the capsule to bring the gate upward. Slide the compass along the ruler to map margin for accurate alignment of lines. Ignore the needle. Double-check: the gate must be up.

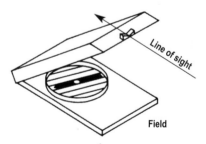

Figure 7.9 Use the compass with the mirror sight. Holding the compass at eye level, turn your body until the needle is boxed. Line of sight now points at the destination. Double-check: the needle's North end must be in the gate.

Basic Procedure for Taking a Bearing

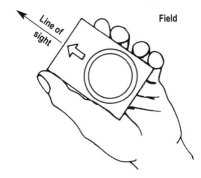

Figure 7.10 Aim the direction-of-travel arrow at a mapped target. Ignore capsule and needle. Double-check: the arrow must point at the target.

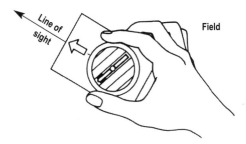

Figure 7.11 While aiming the compass at the target, turn the capsule until the needle is boxed. Double-check: the needle's North end must be in the gate.

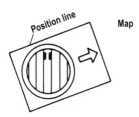

Figure 7.12 Place the compass with gate upward on the map so that the known point, your position or a target, is on one long edge. Turn the entire compass to make the lines parallel to left or right map margin. The edge in the direction of the arrow now points to the target, in the direction opposite to your position.

More Accurate Procedure for Taking a Bearing

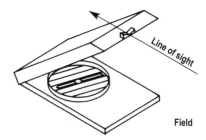

Figure 7.13 Use the mirror sight. Aim at the mapped target. While keeping the object in sight, turn the capsule until the North end of the needle is boxed.

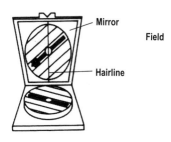

Figure 7.14 With the target in the sight and the needle boxed, the hairline in the mirror must seem to pass through the exact center of the compass.

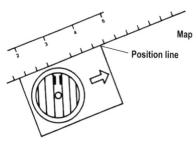

Figure 7.15 Use a ruler along the compass to make the lines in the capsule, with gate up, parallel with left or right map margin, and to connect the known point—your position or target—and the unknown one. The direction-of-travel arrow points at your target; your position is in the opposite direction.

8.

Magnetic Direction

You know that maps show true directions. You also already know that in most places compasses point not to true North (geographic North), but somewhat off to one side or the other—a fact known at least since the mid-fifteenth century. *Declination* is the angle between true North and magnetic North. Sailors call it *variation*.

In the contiguous United States the declination varies from 18° West of true North in the Northeast (Maine) to 19° East of true North in the Northwest (Washington) (see Figure 8.1). In either place, if you ignored the declination, you'd be about 2,000 feet off for every mile traveled (350 meters for every kilometer). And every bearing you took would be off by the same distance for every mile or kilometer between you and your target.

To help you remember: that error works out to 100 feet per degree per mile. In metric units it is—not quite so neatly—18 meters per degree per kilometer.

Magnetic Poles

You may have learned in elementary school that a compass needle points to the magnetic North Pole, which is some distance from the geographic North Pole. The geographic North Pole, from which all meridians radiate, gives the direction of true North anywhere on earth.

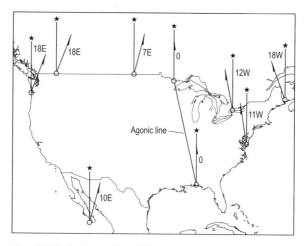

Figure 8.1 Declination at selected U.S. locations. Line with star indicates true North; line with arrow indicates the direction of the compass needle at each location (magnetic North). The angle between the two is the declination.

You may also have come across a map of the United States that tried to show the difference between true North and the direction of a compass needle by a series of lines (see Figure 8.2). (The first deviation map was published in 1701 based on the work of Sir Edward Halley.)

One line, marked zero—connecting the western end of Lake Superior and the lower tip of Mississippi—is known as the *agonic* line. Along that line the declination is zero, meaning there is no angle between true and magnetic North. The other lines, connecting places where the angle is the same, are known as *isogonic* lines, or simply *isogonics*.

A casual glance shows that the eastern lines are labeled "West"; the ones west of the agonic line are labeled "East." All converge toward the top of the map. But, contrary to what you have been taught, they don't run directly toward magnetic North.

Almost everything you have learned about this subject is grossly misleading, if not downright false. The only claim that has merit is that the magnetic North Pole is some distance from the geographic pole.

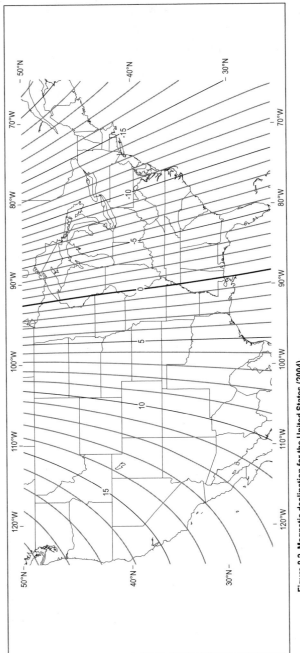

Figure 8.2 Magnetic declination for the United States (2004).

Contrary to what teachers and instruction sheets may tell you, compass needles do *not* point to the magnetic North Pole. And the relation between the two poles has little to do with the declination of a given place.

Nowhere does the agonic line follow that meridian (see Figure 8.3). In the Americas it steers a course of about 15° east of south at first, gradually increasing that angle to 25°. No point of South America is within 1,000 miles of the 103rd meridian. But the agonic line enters that continent near Quito, Ecuador, and leaves it near Viedma, Argentina, at longitude 63°W! (That's about 2,300 miles [3,600 kilometers] from the meridian that connects the magnetic and geographic poles.)

The agonic line through North and South America about which you just read is a model of conformity compared to its other arm, which enters Europe on a civilized southerly course in Scandinavia and leaves it near Toulon, France. It swings through Algeria, to Central Africa, then veers up toward Karachi and New Delhi. It then turns through China and Mongolia, then almost due north through Russia into the Arctic Ocean, then loops back south through the Philippines, west to Vietnam, and across to Indonesia and westernmost Australia to the magnetic South Pole.

You don't need to dust off your globe to see that this is not a line dictated by the position of the geographic or magnetic poles.

Other isogonic lines are no better behaved. A gaggle of them form a closed pattern around Verkhoyansk in northeastern Siberia at roughly 67′N and 133′E, like the isobars of a gigantic high-pressure area. (Coincidentally, this is also the coldest city on Earth, where the average temperature in January is −48°F [−44°C] and the temperature bottomed out at −90°F [−68°C] for two days in 1892. Temperatures reached 104°F [40°C] in July 1998, also giving Verkhoyansk credit for world's widest temperature range.)

Fortunately, there's a rather simple conclusion to all this for readers in the United States and Canada. Once you know, however roughly, where the agonic line runs across the continent, you'll always have a

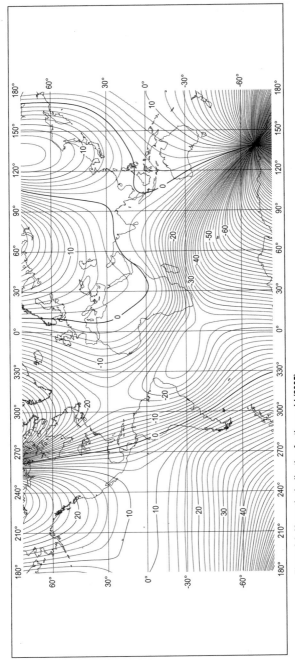

Figure 8.3 Magnetic declination for the world (2005).

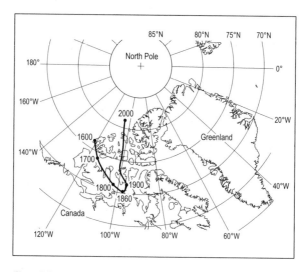

Figure 8.4 Movement of magnetic North Pole over 400 years.

check on whether the declination is East or West. In the White Mountains and the Appalachians, it must be West; in the Rockies, it's East.

Change in Declination

Scientists now believe the magnetic poles have reversed polarity (North becoming South) about twenty-five times in the past five million years. The most recent flip was 720,000 years ago, and another is sure to happen.

The magnetic North Pole has also wandered over a wide area in the recent past (see Figure 8.4). This *secular variation* is caused by the rolling motion of the Earth's liquid iron core and electric currents. The magnetic North Pole currently moves about 25 miles (40 kilometers) to the northwest per year. In May 2001, the magnetic North Pole was in the Arctic Ocean at latitude 81.3°N and longitude 110.8°W. By 2005, it was predicted to be at 82.7°N and 114.4°W.

When the magnetic South Pole was reached for the first time in 1908 by Shackleton's expedition, it was located at 71.6°S and 152°E. By 2000, it was in the Southern Ocean at 64.7°S and 138.0°E and moving 6 to 9 miles (10 to 15 kilometers) northwesterly each year.

When you're standing at the geographic North Pole, your compass will point South toward the magnetic pole. If you were to stand at the magnetic pole with a compass, harder done than said, the needle would try to point downward.

Anyone who wants to can find the declination for any particular location on the planet by going online. Government websites for both Canada and the United States offer declination calculators that let you enter coordinates and even years (search for Geological Survey of Canada: Geomagnetism and NOAA's National Geodetic Data Center). Most GPS units are programmed until at least 2010 for magnetic declination (this information comes from a built-in table, not satellites). Even some instruction sheets for compasses include isogonic maps.

When our Fall River Pass map was published in 1958, the declination was 15°E. In 1977, the map was photorevised and the declination updated to 13°E. In 2005, it was down to 10.5°E.

London is often used as an example of this phenomenon (see Table 8.1), because of the accurate records available there. Note that not only has the magnitude of declination changed, but also the direction.

It's also worth noting that there can be local anomalies that are not accounted for. Although rare, the difference can be dramatic—one area in Minnesota is off by 16°E with anomalies just a few miles away of 12°W.

Declination from Map & Compass

Perhaps surprisingly, the most accurate method for determining local declination is finding it yourself. Even the U.S. Geological Survey states that "there is no better way to obtain the magnetic declination; anything else published is an approximation of this method." All you need is a detailed map, on a scale of, say, 1:24,000, 1:25,000, 1:50,000, or 1:62,500, and a compass.

Table 8.1 Change in declination at London, England, since 1600

Year	Declination	Mean annual change
1600	8°E	8′W
1650	1°E	10′W
1700	7°W	13′W
1750	18°W	7′W
1800	24°W	2′E
1850	22°W	7′E
1900	16°W	10′E
1950	8°W	4′E
1980	6°W	8′E
2000	3°W	

If you use a compass that you just point for taking bearings, don't bother with this method. If, however, you have no knowledge of local declination, even a simple compass can give you at least an idea of its magnitude and direction.

One recommended procedure has you orient your map along a mapped straight line—a road, railroad, telephone line, or pipeline. Orienting a map, you'll recall, means making the upper edge of the map face true North.

First you use your compass to get approximate North. When the image on the map is parallel to the straight line in the landscape, the map is oriented.

Cautions: On roads, a power line or telephone line close by may affect your compass. Railroad tracks, unless stripped of rails and wires, and pipelines are also likely to deflect the needle. The trick then is to work parallel to, rather than right on top of, these reference lines.

When you have the map oriented by the straight line, place your compass (travel arrow facing North) with one of its long edges along the right or left margin of the map, and box the needle.

If the declination is West, you can read it directly off the degree scale on your compass. For example, when you read 10°, the declination here and now is 10°W. When you read a figure somewhat below 360°, such as 350°, subtract it from 360° and label it East; in this case, 10°E.

If you didn't research the area you're visiting ahead of time, this method is useful on old maps that give no hint of the local declination. It could be 1° or 20°, east or west, so knowing where your needle points is important.

Another method requires two known, mapped points rather than a straight line. In the mountains, pairs of such points are easier to find than straight lines. And they won't distract your compass.

When you have found the two points—say the trail crossing where you are and an unmistakable peak—on the map, work out the course from where you are to the other point. Work as accurately as you can, using the ruler as described in Chapter 7.

Then take the bearing of the second point. Say you get a bearing of 55°, and the course came out as 45°. The difference between the (true) course and the (magnetic) bearing is 10°. Label the difference—the local declination—West when the bearing is greater than the course, as in this example. If the numbers were switched, you'd label it East.

If your compass has an adjustment to allow for declination, it must be set to zero while you work out what the declination is, unless you just want to check that you have set it right.

Declination from Polaris

Polaris, the North Star, gives another way to get a bearing (0°) to check on declination.

Most people in the Northern Hemisphere know how to find Polaris from the Big Dipper. And from Polaris, on any clear night, you can determine North. The Big Dipper method of finding Polaris is illustrated in Figure 12.2.

Look at the northern sky. There, as many degrees above the horizon as you are north of the equator, you will find Polaris. If you're near latitude 40°N, it will be 40° above the horizon. With your arm outstretched, a spread hand from thumb to little finger measures about 20° in the sky; a fist, thumb showing, covers 10°; each finger, about 2°. So in latitude 40°N, Polaris will be about two spread hands above the horizon.

Polaris is a second-magnitude star, which means it remains visible even when the moon is full. There is no equally bright or brighter star nearby to confuse you. (Planets don't get to that part of the sky.)

Polaris is about midway between the Big Dipper's guide stars and the constellation Cassiopeia. That's the one that looks to some people like a chair, to most of us like a sloppy capital letter *M* or *W*, depending on which side is up.

So now you have three ways to find or check on Polaris and find the celestial North Pole.

Declination from the Map

Don't rely on any published map without applying the change in declination.

Topo map users in the United States, if they are aware of declination, rely on the diagram printed on the popular 7½′ maps (see Figure 8.5).

The diagram gives the declination in figures (to the nearest half degree) and shows the direction in which the magnetic needle (MN) of a compass points in relation to true North, which is always given straight up and is indicated by a line ending in a star.

Here are several warnings from the U.S. Geological Survey on the use of this diagram:

1. The angle between the lines gives the direction (here East) of the declination, not necessarily the correct number of degrees. You get those from the printed number.
2. The value is for the year given and will have changed since then.
3. The declination given refers to the center of the sheet. This has little importance for outdoor sports

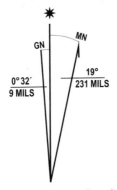

UTM grid and 1977 magnetic north
declination at center of sheet

Figure 8.5 Declination diagram.

and travel. Where the lines are closest, in the eastern United States, the declination changes at most by 1° in 50 miles. So on any of these topographic quads the value is virtually the same anywhere on the map.

4. There might be some local magnetic attraction. Though there are thousands of local anomalies, it's not likely that you'll be misled by that phenomenon, since most are very weak. There are a handful of spots, however, that can render a compass useless.

Grid North (GN) is primarily used by surveyors. It refers to the direction of meridians on maps that take in much more territory than our topo maps (4° latitude by 6° longitude on a scale of 1:1,000,000). Our map is in Zone 13 of that series of maps; that zone stretches from longitude 102°W to longitude 108°W. Its central meridian (105°W) is drawn running due North, and all other meridians of that zone are drawn parallel to it.

The central meridian of the sheet from which our map is cut (105°48′45″W) is drawn pointing due North. Since meridians converge toward the pole, that meridian must make a small angle with the UTM grid of Zone 13. That's the angle referred to in the figure, 0°32′.

The left and right map margins, which we used for aligning the meridian lines in the compass capsule, are also true meridians. That is, they run to true North exactly. Thus, our topo quads are a trifle narrower at top than at bottom. The difference is not noticeable until you put the top and bottom edges together.

Allowing for Declination

Say you know what the declination is in your area of operation. What do you do with that information?

You have four choices:

1. You can ignore it—sometimes.
2. If your compass has an adjustment for declination, set it and forget about it until you move on to an area with different declination.
3. Draw lines on your map and use them in place of the map margins to align the meridian lines in your compass capsule.
4. Add the declination to or subtract it from the figures shown on the 360° scale of your compass. The rules about when to add and when to subtract are easy to learn, but just as easy to mix up.

Ignoring Declination

In a few operations you can ignore the declination, however large it may be.

Walking a field bearing, for example. Whatever correction you should apply to the bearing is cancelled by the correction to be applied to the course to be walked.

There are a few operations in which a small error hardly matters. Orienting a map, for example. Once you have it approximately lined up for North on top, you can spot some prominent object. You then ignore any small error and adjust by a tug at the corner of the map rather than by compass work.

Finding a mapped mountain peak in the landscape and identifying one on the map are similar to orienting the map and require only low accuracy.

Deciding which fork in a road or trail to take doesn't require a high degree of accuracy. And probably nobody would worry about declination for stringing a laundry line to catch the morning sun.

Bearings taken for fixing your position require the greatest accuracy and if taken with a mirror-type (or optical sighting) compass should be corrected even for minimal declination.

The use of declination also depends on the terrain. For example, a rough course will get you close enough to a lake to see it and correct your heading. You may want to be more accurate when you're trying to reach the only bridge over a ravine or a single ford through a stream. (Chapter 13 describes a useful trick for such situations.) And when dragging yourself to your water cache in the desert, you'll want all the accuracy you can squeeze out of your compass (or a GPS unit).

Even the weather may influence your choice of ignoring the declination or correcting for it. For example, what was a well-beaten trail yesterday has been obliterated by snow. Blazes and color markings are hard to spot. Even cairns are hiding. To add to the fun you can expect a whiteout at any time. Accurate compass work will be essential without a functioning GPS unit.

Mechanical Adjustment

The easiest way to correct for declination is to use a compass that lets you set the declination and forget it. That feature adds a few dollars to the cost of the compass, but the peace of mind is well worth it.

The mechanism for making the adjustment is similar in all the compasses. You offset the boxing mark—the orienting arrow, gate, slot, or whatever device is used for boxing the needle.

After adjustment, the boxed compass needle does not run parallel to the orienting lines in the capsule but makes an angle with them toward either the East or the West.

That's achieved by a double bottom. A clearly marked scale lets you shift the boxing mark in relation to the capsule lines for exactly the amount and direction of the declination.

As explained in Chapter 6, the offset can be controlled by a miniature screwdriver or some other means. The effect of all these mechanisms is the same. Some are easier on your fingers than others, but you shouldn't need to adjust it often.

However, don't forget to adjust your compass settings in an area of different declination. If you make a habit of checking the declination every time you open a new map, you won't forget. You shouldn't need to adjust your compass for adjoining map sheets used during a trip. But if you don't reset the compass when beginning a new trip in a new area, your compass readings may be inaccurate.

Once the compass is set for the area of your activity, you can work all the routines described in Chapter 7 as if there were no such thing as declination.

Lining the Map

Another method sometimes recommended for allowing for declination is to line the entire map with waterproof ink, inclining the lines at the angle and direction of the declination. These lines, called *magnetic meridians,* show how a compass needle would point in the map area.

With these lines drawn on the map, you don't need rules or arithmetic. You use the magnetic meridians to align the meridians on the bottom of the capsule. And you don't have to move the compass along a ruler to the margin of the map. In other words, you use the magnetic meridians rather than geographic meridians. Otherwise the instructions remain the same.

This method makes compass use under stress foolproof (provided you keep the boxing mark in the capsule upward on the map), which is why maps for orienteering competitions are printed with lines in this fashion.

To catch at least one line in the capsule, the drawn lines must be no more than 1 to 1½ inches (25 to 37 millimeters) apart. On the quad from which our map is taken, that means eighteen lines up to 2 feet (60 centimeters) long must be drawn fastidiously.

While nice in theory, this is such a tedious process that almost nobody will bother. If you need this option, perhaps for using an orienteering compass, a computer with digital mapping software can print maps with magnetic declination lines.

Correction by Arithmetic

The last method for adjusting for declination costs nothing and requires no drawing. But it takes some figure work and four rules.

Until now we have hardly ever read the degree scale of the compass. We have taken courses off the map and walked them, or taken bearings and plotted them on the map, without ever reading the numbers on the dial.

Those happy days are over. To use this method, you must read the dial, and you must add or subtract the declination. Obviously, different rules for adding and subtracting are required, depending on whether the declination is easterly or westerly.

But that's not all. For each declination, we'll need different rules for working from map to landscape (for example, taking a course off the map and then finding the compass setting to follow) and from landscape to map (for example, plotting a bearing).

Fortunately, you are not likely to jump back and forth from easterly declination to westerly. If you hike only in the Rockies, you'll never have to bother about westerly declination; if you hike the Appalachian Trail, you won't have to bother about easterly declination. (Don't worry about what happens when you cross the zero declination line—nothing happens. If you approach it from the West, the declination goes from an unimportant ½° East to nothing. And after you have hiked perhaps another 50 miles it becomes a still-trivial ½° West.)

Unfortunately, the rules sound very much alike, so the danger of getting the wrong one is greater. When you use the wrong rule—by adding when you should be subtracting, or the other way around—you double the error of declination.

Again using our map as an example (declination 10.5°E), you'd be 21° off. For every mile you walk in what you think is the right direction, you go almost a half mile into the hinterlands.

One way to remember the rules is to write them, perhaps abbreviated and including only the ones you need on a particular trip, on a card and glue it to your compass.

If you operate only in East declination—that is, in the western United States or western Canada—you need only two rules: one for map-to-field conversion, and the other for field-to-map. Your card will read as follows:

Map-to-field: Subtract declination (Variation East, turn dial East)

Field-to-map: Add declination (Variation East, turn dial West)

Taking a course or the direction of some feature off the map for walking, or locating the feature in the landscape, is map-to-field: subtract.

Taking a bearing with the compass and plotting it on the map for identification, or to get a position line, is field-to-map: add.

There are a few tricks you should remember when you're doing the arithmetic. A circle consists of 360°. If after adding you get a figure larger than that, say 370°, subtract 360°; you'll get 10°.

If you must subtract a declination larger than the dial reading, borrow 360° and add it to the dial reading. If the dial reads 10° and the declination to be subtracted is 12°, figure 10 + 360 = 370; 370 − 12 = 358. The answer is 358°.

In the first example, you would have set the compass capsule until 10° was at the index mark; in the second, until it showed 358°.

When you get good at this sort of thing you can just turn the capsule the correct number of degrees in the right direction. Then you don't need the 360° gimmicks. By turning the dial clockwise (East), you subtract; by turning it the other way, you add. You don't have to memorize that; you can see it on the compass scale.

The danger in the turn-the-dial method is that after starting you may forget where the dial was originally.

Here are two examples for easterly declination 12°.

Example 1. After you place your compass from start to destination and align the capsule with the map margin, the dial reads 180°. This is map-to-field, so you must subtract. You should get 168° either by arithmetic or by turning the capsule clockwise 12°. You now box the needle and walk in the direction indicated by the arrow.

Example 2. After you take a bearing and box the needle, the dial of your compass reads 90°. This is field-to-map, so you must add. You should get 102° either by arithmetic or by turning the capsule counterclockwise 12°. You now align the lines in the capsule with the left or right margin of the map and are ready to plot the bearing on the map.

If you operate only in West declination—that is, in the eastern United States or eastern Canada—you again need only two rules: one for map-to-field, and one for field-to-map. Your card will read as follows:

Map-to-field: Add declination (Variation West, turn dial West)

Field-to-map: Subtract declination (Variation West, turn dial East)

Taking a course or the direction of some feature off the map for walking, or locating the feature in the landscape, is map-to-field: add.

Taking a bearing with the compass and plotting it on the map for identification, or to get a position line, is field-to-map: subtract.

Here are two examples for westerly declination 12°.

Example 1. After you place your compass from start to destination and align the capsule with the vertical map margin, the dial reads 180°. That's map-to-field, so you must add. You should get 192° either by arithmetic or by turning the capsule counterclockwise 12°. You now box the needle and walk in the direction indicated by the arrow.

Example 2. After you take a bearing and box the needle, the dial of your compass reads 90°. That's field-to-map, so you must subtract. You should get 78° either by arithmetic or by turning the capsule clockwise 12°.

Handling sums larger than 360° or subtracting declinations larger than the dial reading is of course the same as described above for easterly declination. Also, for both East and West declination, turning the dial clockwise, toward East, subtracts; turning the dial counterclockwise, toward West, adds.

Perhaps now you'll decide to get a compass with built-in adjustment for declination.

9.

Altimeter Navigation

An altimeter can add another dimension to your navigation—height.

Topographic maps, though themselves flat, indicate heights. Using an instrument that measures heights, we can improve our ability to fix our position—at least in hilly or mountainous country. (When you are hiking in the Everglades in southern Florida, where the land slopes perhaps a dozen feet in 100 miles, knowing your height to the nearest 10 feet would not help your navigation.)

All altimeters—whether analog or digital—are cousins of barometers. Like barometers, they measure local air pressure by weighing a column of air that extends to space. Since air pressure diminishes the higher you go, altimeter dials can be calibrated for reading elevations in either feet or meters.

For flying, portable altimeters indicate the cabin pressure, so your instrument may read 7,500 feet (2,300 meters) while the plane is flying at 30,000 feet (10 kilometers).

Simple Uses for Altimeters

Even the least accurate altimeters, whether analog or digital, have their uses in mountain navigation: they let you estimate your progress.

If you know you face a 4,000-foot climb, an indication on your altimeter of 2,000 feet above the valley tells you half the climb is behind you. If you had set the starting elevation to zero, it would now indicate 2,000 feet.

If the rest of the climb is not much steeper—the lines on the topo map are not closer together—and if the footway doesn't deteriorate, you can estimate your time of arrival. Add a little more time for the next 2,000 feet to allow for fatigue, a stop to get water, shade, a boulder to rest your pack on, vistas, rare flowers, or any other excuse to pause or rest.

On the way down, rests are usually in less demand. But you can still track your progress. Before starting back, set the altimeter to 4,000 feet, for example. When the needle indicates 3,000, you are a quarter of the way down, at 2,000, halfway down, and so on.

An inexpensive analog altimeter is usually calibrated in 100-foot or 20-meter intervals, which lets you estimate your gain or loss of elevation to 50 feet or 10 meters. That's certainly adequate for roughly checking your progress and estimating your time of arrival.

You can't expect much more for $60. But people do. And that's why many outdoor books either don't talk about altimeters at all or warn that they are not much use "because they are influenced by the weather." They are, but that's not why the inexpensive altimeters will not help you in precision navigation.

The limitation lies in their simple construction. The heart of mechanical altimeters—and barometers—is a copper capsule that has very low air pressure inside (a near vacuum). When the external pressure drops or increases, the walls move out or in a few thousandths of an inch. The needle of the altimeter or barometer shows the movements of the capsule, much magnified.

Digital altimeters use an electronic pressure transducer, which consists of a silicon wafer bonded to a metal diaphragm. Fluctuations in air pressure deflect the diaphragm, causing changes in the electrical characteristics of the wafer that give the reading.

Unfortunately, the capsule or metal diaphragm also expands when it gets warmer and contracts when

Figure 9.1 Thommen TX altimeters are temperature compensated and available in several upper ranges, with escalating prices. Model TX-18 (3.2 ounces, $322), shown here, has a range of 21,000 feet, calibrated at 20-foot intervals. The TX series is accurate to within 30 feet over the entire range if used correctly and will last many lifetimes; no batteries required.

it gets chilled. The inexpensive altimeter magnifies these changes. For example, in simulating the temperature in one's shirt pocket, decreasing the temperature from 80°F (27°C) to 45°F (7°C) causes a rise of 400 to 450 feet (130 meters). Similarly, raising the temperature from 20°F (−7°C) to 45°F can lower the reading by up to 600 feet (180 meters).

Choosing an Altimeter

When you're deciding on an altimeter, the first consideration is whether to go analog or digital. Unless you just want a toy, don't waste your money on a mechanical altimeter that costs less than a good pair of boots.

For navigational purposes, the only mechanical altimeter worth considering is the German-built Peet Brothers Model 88, which runs around $200, or one of the Swiss-made Thommen TX series (seven models), which cost well over $300 (see Figure 9.1). These are remarkable precision instruments with sixteen to nine-

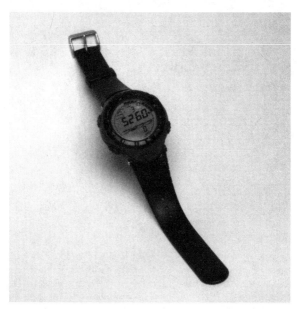

Figure 9.2 The Suunto Advizor wristop computer (1.8 ounces, $300) is an altimeter, compass, and heart rate monitor (requires chest strap), as well as a watch.

teen jeweled bearings and sophisticated temperature compensation. These will never let you down, since they need no batteries, and make good heirlooms for the great-grandkids.

For most outdoor users, however, it makes more sense to get an electronic altimeter that is worn on the wrist (see Figure 9.2) or built into one of their other gadgets (anemometer [see Figure 9.3], bike computer, GPS). The price of these has dropped significantly, and they are becoming more ubiquitous.

Look for a model with a resolution of 10 feet (5 meters) or better; some offer 3-foot (1-meter) increments but this won't improve your navigating. Make certain the altimeter has a backlight so you can read it easily at night. An altimeter alarm that goes off when you reach a set altitude can be useful at times. Models that have a built-in compass provide a quick bearing check, though they should not be considered replace-

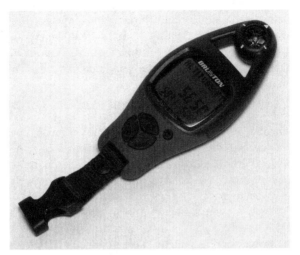

Figure 9.3 The Brunton Atmospheric Data Center Pro (1.8 ounces, $250) measures altitude, wind speed, humidity, and temperature.

ments for a real compass with a sighting mirror. An easily changeable battery is a huge plus.

If you are a skier, you may want a model that counts the number of runs, measures the speed of descent, and tallies the amount of vertical skied in a day or week. Note that this trivia often wears thin on those around you who are less number driven.

Be warned: just because a digital altimeter has a thermometer does *not* mean it is temperature compensated. Most models do not exchange information between altimeter and thermometer. This deficit is rarely mentioned in reviews, and it takes a close read of the manual or website to find out whether the altimeter is actually temperature compensated; suspect that it is not, unless it is specifically mentioned. This may not be a problem when the altimeter is worn on the wrist since body heat reduces fluctuations. But removing the altimeter, or wearing it on very cold days, can throw the reading off by several hundred feet.

A GPS receiver alone is not a substitute for an altimeter. Many GPS units have built-in atmospheric altimeters for greater accuracy. A few exchange data between the receiver and altimeter to compensate for changing weather. If your GPS lacks an altimeter, you will likely want a separate altimeter for navigating in the mountains; these often have additional capabilities.

Basic Altimeter Navigation

Theoretically, temperature compensation means the reading will not change when you warm or cool the instrument. Mechanical altimeters use a beryllium-copper bimetal to achieve this, while digital models use a computer.

For such instruments, it is worthwhile to check into the influence of moving weather systems on the altimeter reading. (Inexpensive analog altimeters, on the other hand, are not sensitive enough to small changes to worry about short-term—say hourly—weather influences.)

If you have watched barometers regularly, you'll seldom have seen movements of more than 1 inch, or 25 millimeters, of mercury (34 millibars) in twenty-four hours. That works out to 0.04 inch (1 millimeter) of mercury, or about 1½ millibars, per hour, which translates into about 40 feet (12 meters) in elevation difference at 3,000 feet (1,000 meters) above sea level (a little less, lower down; somewhat more, higher up).

On most days, the hourly change in barometric pressure, and with it the elevation error, is minimal. But we should not neglect it with an instrument that's capable of giving accurate readings over a wide range of temperatures.

Minimizing errors from changing weather requires a simple procedure: At the trailhead, set the altimeter as accurately as possible to the elevation read from the map. From here on, the altimeter should show about the same elevation above sea level as your map does.

Whenever you come to a mapped point you can positively identify, reset the altimeter for the elevation given for that point. It could be at a side creek joining the creek you're following, a bridge, a saddle or peak, or a power line crossing your trail.

Once you start looking for them, you'll find such resetting points all the time. The more frequent you calibrate, the better. Ideally, you should keep vertical distance between resettings to 1,600 feet (500 meters) and the horizontal distance to 6 miles (10 kilometers).

But say you have walked off trail for one hour without having been able to reset your elevation from the map.

As we have seen, it would be unusual for the weather to have fooled you by more than 40 feet (12 meters). In the mountains, 40 feet is the usual contour interval on 7½′ topo quads. On a mapped trail, therefore, you'd know your position within one contour line. What more can you expect with so little effort in navigation?

Here's an example: you're climbing the La Poudre Pass Trail, which takes off near the western border of section 7 on our map. You would have set your altimeter where the trail—at first a light-duty road—branches off from the medium-duty (red) road. There's a bench mark giving an elevation of 9,095 feet just south of the branch-off, and the side road immediately crosses the 9,080 contour, so you would have set your altimeter to 9,080 feet.

Now you are in the trees, and your altimeter reads 9,280 feet. Where are you?

You have two position lines. One is the La Poudre Pass Trail. The other is the 9,280 contour line. You must be at or near the point where the two position lines cross, not far from the northeast corner of section 1.

Since you probably have been under way for less than an hour, the error from change in barometric pressure due to a weather system is not likely to be significant; within a one-half contour interval.

Another example: you are driving east along Trail Ridge Road looking for the start of the Ute Trail near the lower center of our cutout.

"Have we passed it?"

Nobody in the car has counted curves, but you recall having checked the altimeter where you saw the

La Poudre Pass Trail branch off. It read, just as you had expected, about 9,100 feet. It now reads 9,900 feet.

One glance at the map and you can confidently announce, "No, we have some more climbing to do." You have not even reached the 10,000-foot contour, and the trail takes off between that and the 10,200-foot line.

By the way, the confidence in altimeter readings not changing much in one hour refers to observers moving slowly, on foot or perhaps by canoe or kayak. In an automobile, you may approach a high- or low-pressure area fast enough to make hourly resettings of the altimeter too far apart.

As navigator on this road, be sure to check and if necessary reset the altimeter at Milner Pass.

Here are a few more examples, illustrated by the contour map in Figure 9.4.

Example 1. You have set your altimeter at the confluence of two branches of a creek at point 1 near the road crossing. A bench mark there reads 3,120 feet on the map. On the original map, which showed contours every 40 feet, you could also have found the elevation from the contour lines. (To keep matters simple, only the index contours at 200-foot intervals are shown.)

Example 2. You have worked your way up the northern branch of the creek. Your altimeter now reads 3,800 feet. You are at the crossing of two position lines—the mapped creek and the contour line; you must be at or near point 2.

Example 3. You are on the trail that enters near the southwestern corner of the map. Your altimeter now indicates 3,600 feet. You must be at or near the intersection of two position lines—the trail and the 3,600-foot elevation, point 3.

Example 4. You know how to fix your position from two compass bearings. They may be hard to come by in a forest where you'd be lucky to get an occasional glimpse of even one identifiable landmark. That'd be enough on a mapped trail, but here you have been bushwhacking. Now you get a glimpse of the fire tower on the next mountain. Corrected for declination, it bears 80°. Your altimeter now reads 3,800 feet. You

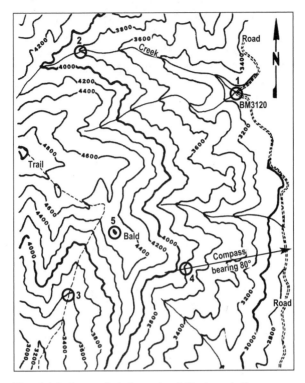

Figure 9.4 Contour map for text examples of altimeter navigation.

plot the bearing, your first position line, then look for the 3,800-foot contour. You are where the two position lines—bearing and contour—cross, at or near point 4.

Note: you get the most reliable fix from a compass bearing at right angles to your trail. In the same way you get the best fix when the compass bearing crosses the contour line at about that angle.

You might think you could just as well be near point 3. But look closer; you would certainly know whether the higher ground was toward the west, as at point 4, or toward the north, as at point 3. You could not see the fire tower from point 3 because the mountain you're standing on is in the way.

Example 5. You are again on the trail used in example 3. You see the open area, locally known as a bald, near point 5. You climb it for the view. Glancing at the map, you notice it's the only isolated spot in the area that rises to 4,600 feet. The sharp bend in the trail that you can see from your lookout makes you quite sure you've got the right point. Reset your altimeter here to 4,600 feet.

Example 6. While you're standing at point 5, the clouds roll in and obscure your view. You decide to descend out of the storm and then contour around the mountain to your gear cache at point 4. Set the altimeter alarm to 3,800 feet and head downhill to the east. When the alarm beeps, turn right and stay on that contour until you reach your gear.

Effects of Nonstandard Air Temperatures

When you do try your altimeter, you'll find that your navigation doesn't turn out quite as neatly as the examples.

If you use an altimeter that's said to be temperature compensated and easily read to the nearest 10 feet (3 meters), you'll find at each resetting point that your instrument is somewhat off. Even in settled weather, when experience tells you that the barometric pressure can't have changed significantly in the hour since you last reset the altimeter, it will not quite agree with the elevation on the map.

That's not the fault of the altimeter. It'd be a coincidence if the altimeter did read exactly right.

This has nothing to do with inadequate temperature compensation. There is a fundamental reason for even the very best altimeters to seem somewhat off. It has to do with the atmosphere itself.

Altimeters are designed, built, and tested according to a theoretical atmosphere in which the air pressure diminishes in a certain way while at the same time the temperature drops steadily as you go higher up.

The sea-level temperature in that atmosphere is assumed to be 59°F (15°C) and to drop steadily by 3.6°F per 1,000 feet (6.5°C per 1,000 meters) in the altitudes that interest us. It is most unlikely that on any given day the air temperature where you are is exactly what the standard calibration of altimeters assumes it to be.

A perfectly temperature-compensated mechanical altimeter ignores the local temperature. But the column of air that weighs down on the barometric cell in your instrument does not. It is denser (heavier) when it's colder, and thinner (lighter) when it's warmer, than the simple formula assumes.

If the air through which you climbed averaged 20°F warmer than the standard atmosphere shows, the altimeter will indicate about 960 feet gained when it should indicate 1,000 feet.

If the air through which you climbed averaged 20°F cooler than the standard atmosphere shows, the altimeter will indicate a gain of about 1,040 feet.

Metric examples: if the air was 10°C warmer than the standard atmosphere assumes, the altimeter will indicate a gain of 965 meters when it should show a gain of 1,000 meters. If the air was 10°C cooler than the standard atmosphere assumes, it will indicate a gain of about 1,035 meters.

When you are going down, the altimeter will act in the same erroneous manner as it did on the way up. That has to be so; if you ran up and down the same vertical distance, the altimeter should show the same reading at the end of your trip as at the start.

When the air is *warmer* than standard, the altimeter *underestimates* the *change* in elevation (up or down).

When the air is *cooler* than standard, the altimeter *overestimates* the *change* in elevation (up or down).

The error encountered when you are climbing is quite straightforward. But when you are going down it is a bit tricky. Assume in the first example (air warmer than standard) that you were starting out downhill from 1,000 feet. At sea level, having been carried down

Table 9.1 Standard atmosphere, temperatures used in calibrating altimeters

English units		Metric units	
Elevation (feet)	Temperature (°F)	Elevation (meters)	Temperature (°C)
Sea level	59	Sea level	15
2,000	52.1	500	11.9
4,000	44.8	1,000	8.7
6,000	37.6	1,500	5.4
8,000	30.5	2,000	2.2
10,000	23.4	2,500	−1.1
12,000	16.2	3,000	−4.4
14,000	9.1	3,500	−7.6
16,000	1.8	4,000	−10.9
18,000	−5.1	4,500	−14.1
20,000	−12.3	5,000	−17.4
22,000	−19.3	5,500	−20.6
24,000	−26.5	6,000	−23.9
26,000	−33.6	7,000	−30.4
28,000	−40.8	8,000	−36.9

1,000 feet, your altimeter will show only a 960-foot drop and indicate an elevation of 40 feet above sea level.

It's shy 40 feet going up or going down. But the elevation indicated is too low going up, too high going down.

Table 9.1 will help give you a feel for whether local temperature is warmer or cooler than the corresponding standard atmosphere temperature.

Here is the discrepancy you can expect for nonstandard temperatures:

For every 1°F, expect a 2-foot error for every 1,000-foot change in elevation.

For every 1°C, expect a 4-meter error for every 1,000-meter change in elevation.

As an example, we'll climb the Red Mountain Trail on a warm summer day with an average temperature of 73°F (it might have started at 58°F and heated up to 88°F), which is 50°F above the standard. If we set our altimeter at 9,080 feet and climb to the Grand Ditch at 10,240 feet, the altimeter should read 10,125 feet (50 × 2 × [1,160 ÷ 1,000] = 116 feet below actual altitude). If you were feeling ambitious on the same day and climbed Shipler Mountain, the altimeter would read 11,090 feet instead of 11,315 feet.

On the other hand, if you enjoy punishment and went up the Red Mountain Trail when it was −27°F, your altimeter should read 10,355 feet.

Altimeters & the Weather

All decent altimeters show barometric pressure. Two different scales are in common use: inches of mercury (inHG) and millibars (mbar).

Barometers are rotten predictors of weather when you are on the move. Unfortunately, there is no simple way to decide what the barometer is doing when you are changing elevation. Even GPS receivers with altimeters have trouble tracking barometric pressure while you are moving.

However, you can achieve good results in forecasting the weather not from the actual barometer reading but from its tendency—whether it is steady, falling, or rising, and how quickly it is changing if it is changing at all. If you are staying in a camp or hut waiting for a storm to clear so you can climb a peak, a quickly rising barometric reading can give you a head start on a weather window.

Or if someone in an expedition base camp is watching the barometer and sees the pressure plummeting and high cirrus clouds moving in, they can radio a warning to climbers on the mountain of an impending storm. If the mercury drops more than 0.05 inHG (1.7 mbar) in three hours, something is probably coming. And if the barometer falls 0.3 inHG (10 mbar) in six hours, the storm is likely big, mean, and almost there.

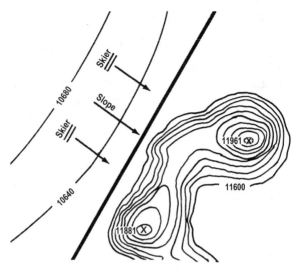

Figure 9.5 Navigation by altimeter and the lay of the land. Left: two skiers determine the slope. Right: terrain where the method would be useful.

While a useful indicator, a barometer is by no means a sure thing when it comes to predicting weather (look how accurate the weather reporters are with Doppler radar and satellite imagery). It often won't warn of the afternoon thunderstorms that are common in the Rockies. And sometimes mountains can create their own weather that isn't associated with a pressure front.

Altimeters & Slope

Another technique for estimating position with an altimeter is based on the lay of the land. When you know approximately where on the map you are, you can sometimes pinpoint your position from the contour line (indicated by your altimeter) and the direction of the slope (from your compass), two position lines.

Figure 9.5 illustrates the idea. The slope is the direction in which water would run. On the map it is the shortest connection from your contour line to the one below (see the top left corner of the sketch).

In the landscape, even in fog, you can simulate your contour line by looking a bit forward or backward and trying to keep some target at the level of your eyes. Then imagine a line drawn between the target and you. Get the direction at right angles to that line, heading down; that's the slope line.

A companion on skis, on snowshoes, or on foot can make it easier to find the contour in the landscape. Have him or her take a position on your level but 30 to 100 feet (10 to 30 meters), depending on visibility, away from you. The slope tends in the direction of a right angle to the line between you.

If you both have compasses, you might make independent estimates of the slope direction as a check.

Now look at the twin peaks illustrated at the bottom right in Figure 9.5.

If your altimeter places you on the 11,600 contour and the slope drops off to the north, you must be north of the 11,961 peak on that line. If the slope tends 270° (west), you are west and a bit south of the peak labeled 11,881. Or you could be west of the 11,961 peak. Another estimate of the slope after a short walk along the contour will let you decide which was the correct position. That method would work nearly everywhere in the vicinity of these peaks.

This won't help you along the side of a long valley, though. You can see that it would not pinpoint your position on our map west of the Colorado in sections 1, 12, and 13, where the contours are almost straight, but it's a technique to keep in mind.

10.

GPS Navigation

For the past millennium, humans have relied on maps and compasses to locate their position on land. Without a compass, and the knowledge of how to use it, staying found could be exceptionally difficult.

But even with a map, compass, and altimeter, finding your way in a snowstorm, in dense fog, or at night can be a real challenge for even the most experienced outdoors person. Without visual clues, it's all too easy to wander about aimlessly or even fall off a cliff.

The age-old methods of navigating began to change on June 16, 1963, when the first operational navigation satellite (part of a system called Transit) was launched by the United States. The system used the Doppler effect from three satellites (plus three spares) in low-altitude (685 miles) polar orbits so that submarines could update their position. Moving objects could be located within 300 feet and fixed targets were determined to 65-foot accuracy. However, the system was slow and had many other drawbacks (it was declassified for civilian use in 1967 but the cost was prohibitive).

In February 1978, the first NAVSTAR (Navigation Satellite Timing and Ranging) satellite was launched into a middle earth orbit (about 12,000 miles up). This marked the start of modern GPS (Global Positioning System) navigation. The Soviet Union began launching

Table 10.1 Global positioning systems

	NAVSTAR	GLONASS	Galileo
No. of satellites:			
	24 + 4	24 + 4	27 + 3
Altitude (km):			
	20,346	19,100	23,616
Altitude (miles):			
	12,642	11,868	14,674
Orbit time:			
	11 hrs. 58 min.	11 hrs. 15 min.	14 hrs. 22 min.
Orbital planes:			
	6	3	3
Inclination:			
	55°	65°	56°
Frequency (MHz):			
	1,227.6	1,246–1,257	1,164–1,300
	1,575.4	1,602–1,616	1,559–1,591

its own version, known as GLONASS (Global Navigation Satellite System), in 1982 (see Table 10.1).

In June 1983, the Department of Defense made its navigation system available to the public. Only two months later, the importance of GPS became apparent when Soviet fighters shot down Korean Air Lines 007 after it strayed off course, killing 269 people, a tragedy that could have been prevented had the plane been equipped with the new technology.

By 1985, eleven of the first-generation (called Block I) satellites encircled the planet and proved the concept was valid. The system became famous during the first Gulf War, when the military scrambled to provide troops with enough receivers.

Since the 1990s, all of the original GPS satellites—often called space vehicles (SV)—have been replaced with twenty-eight second- and third-generation (known as Block II and IIA, which will be phased out) and fourth-generation (Block IIR and IIF) versions. The entire system became fully operational on April 27, 1995, at a cost of roughly $14 billion; upgrades will push the total to $22 billion by 2016.

GPS Basics

It all boils down to really, really big spheres.

In previous chapters, you learned how to determine your position by taking bearings from distant objects and plotting the lines on a map. The intersection of the lines tells you roughly where you are, a process called triangulation. The more position lines you draw and the greater the angles between them, the more accurate your location.

With satellite navigation systems, it's basically the same thing except the receiving unit is taking bearings off objects thousands of miles away that are moving very fast. It's strictly a line-of-sight system, even though the satellites are too far away to actually see. Most things that block your view of the sky will also block the signal.

At least three satellites within view are required for a position fix on a flat map. And a fourth is needed to estimate your elevation. Under ideal circumstances—a clear view of the sky—you can see at least seven satellites greater than 10° above the horizon. But mountains, canyon walls, and trees can interfere with your reading.

With good satellite geometry (widely spaced), a handheld GPS receiver (also called a *GPS unit*) can place you within a 50-foot (15-meter), usually smaller, circle anywhere on the planet with a high degree of accuracy. In all of the continental United States, much of Europe, and portions of Asia near Japan, newer GPS units can receive an additional signal that reduces the circle to a 10-foot (3-meter) circumference. No matter the weather!

How GPS Works

The entire global positioning system comprises three distinct parts: the satellite bubble encircling the earth, a ground control network, and the receivers that interpret the information radioed from above. Although most people refer to a "GPS" as the device they hold in their hands, it's actually a component of a much larger system.

The Russian GLONASS and European Galileo systems work in a similar manner, though there are differences in the details. Presently, none of the consumer-grade GPS receivers are compatible with the other systems, but newer models may someday be multilingual.

The satellite segment consists of twenty-four operating space vehicles, plus three to five backups, that are in six very precise, slightly elliptical orbits, four satellites per orbital plane. The satellites are 12,642 miles (20,346 kilometers) above the earth and traveling at about 8,950 miles per hour (14,400 kilometers per hour); it takes almost 12 hours for them to complete an orbit. From that altitude, seventeen satellites could provide a position anywhere, but the extras help when objects on the ground get in the way.

This fleet of satellites is monitored by stations on Hawaii, a Marshall Island (Kwajalein) in the Pacific Ocean, Diego Garcia in the Indian Ocean, and Ascension Island in the Atlantic Ocean. The master ground station is located at Schriever Air Force Base near Colorado Springs, Colorado. The GPS satellites also detect nuclear blasts, so the mission is doubly vital.

Each satellite sends out signals at two frequencies: 1575.4 MHz (called L1) and 1227.6 MHz (called L2). At present, all civilian receivers pick up only the unencrypted part (the course acquisition [CA] code) of the L1 signal, while military receivers use both the encrypted precision (P) code in the L1 and L2 for more accurate positioning. In the near future, two more signals will be added for civilian purposes, but these are primarily for air traffic control and other commercial applications.

The GPS frequencies were selected because they are not affected by clouds, rain, snow, or other weather conditions. However, the signals will not penetrate water, so a GPS unit will not work underwater and green leaves can block the signal.

A GPS unit cannot be used for locating avalanche victims for several reasons. Tests have shown the signal penetrates only enough to give a lock about 3 feet (1 meter) down, which isn't nearly enough. Also, none of the consumer GPS units are accurate enough to locate a person. And they are too slow for a situation where seconds count.

The GPS signals are broadcast with only 50 watts of power (by comparison, large FM radio stations broadcast at 100,000 watts and your car radio has a hard time just 50 miles (80 kilometers) away). This very weak signal takes about 0.06 second to travel from the satellite to the ground.

Each satellite sends a string of data, called "ephemeris," every 30 seconds about itself and a 12½-minute string, called the "almanac," with information on the entire constellation. Since all of the satellites broadcast on the same frequency, each has its unique identifier code.

The ephemeris gives not only the precise location of the satellite but also the exact time the message was sent. The real trick of the entire system is to accurately measure the time it takes the signal to reach the receiver. This delay is used to calculate the exact distance of each satellite from the receiver. When the distance and position of at least three objects is known, the receiver can tell where it is located by a process called *trilateration*.

Unlike objects on land, however, the satellites are moving rapidly. When the receiver knows the location and distance of a satellite, it is somewhere on the edge of an imaginary sphere that has the satellite in the center and a radius equal to the distance.

Let's say you are 13,000 miles from Satellite A. That knowledge alone doesn't help much, since you could be anywhere on its sphere (see Figure 10.1). But if you also know that you are 15,000 miles from Satellite B, the two spheres overlap and you are somewhere on a plane that cuts the two spheres (see Figure 10.2). Think of the surface created by two soap bubbles that are joined.

This plane is still very big. But if you add a third sphere from Satellite C that is 14,000 miles away, there are only two possible places in the universe that you can be standing (see Figure 10.3). One of these is in

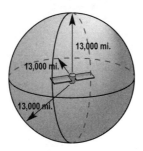

Figure 10.1 The signal from a single GPS satellite locates you somewhere on a sphere of the given radius.

Figure 10.2 With two GPS signals, you are located somewhere on the flat plane where they intersect.

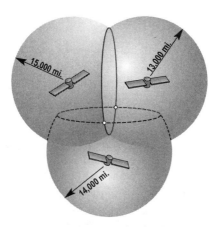

Figure 10.3 Adding a third satellite narrows your position to two points, one of which can be ruled out because it is in outer space.

outer space, so it can be safely discarded. This leaves the spot where you are holding the receiver as the intersection of the three spheres, assuming that the measured distances are correct.

If a satellite's clock was off by as much as a thousandth of a second, the position error would be almost 200 miles; a microsecond error would throw position off by the length of three football fields. Because the timing is critical, each satellite has four atomic clocks on board (two rubidium and two cesium).

While it takes only three satellites to determine your position, the clock in GPS receiving units is nowhere near accurate enough. Therefore, a fourth satellite is required to compare the data and make a correction to the receiver's clock. After you've locked onto four satellites, your GPS unit is accurate to about 340 nanoseconds (0.0000034 second); military units are accurate to 200 nanoseconds. (Because of this precision, GPS is also used for advanced timing applications such as financial transfers.)

It's obvious when the signals reach the receiver. But knowing ahead of time when they will be sent involves more trickery. Suffice to say, the information is part of the code. Subtracting the received and sent times gives the duration. Multiplying this by the speed of light (186,000 miles per second) gives the distance.

Sources of Error

Theoretically, this system would always tell you exactly where you stand. But in reality, there are several sources of error that can mess with you.

The first is user error. Failure to change your GPS receiver to the proper map datum (see Chapter 2) can throw you off as much as 600 feet (180 meters).

The default setting on many GPS units is WGS 84 (World Geodetic System 1984), but most topographic maps in the United States use the NAD 27 CONUS (North American Datum 1927, Continental United States) datum. Recently issued maps use NAD 83, which is the same as WGS 84 for our recreational purposes. Digital maps can be printed with either datum, though WGS 84 is most common. Be sure to check the datum on your maps and set your GPS unit accordingly.

The biggest outside factor is the part of the atmosphere known as the *ionosphere*. We live in the very thin portion called the *troposphere*, which extends from sea level to a bit higher than the summit of Everest, and all of our weather occurs here. Above the troposphere are the stratosphere (12 to 50 kilometers), the mesosphere (50 to 80 kilometers), and the ionosphere (80 to 550 kilometers); beyond that is the exosphere (550 to 10,000 kilometers), which merges with outer space.

The ionosphere is particularly troublesome because it is a layer of ionized air (hence the name) that affects radio signals—loads of free electrons running around bumping into things and slowing them down.

Depending upon conditions, the uncorrected effects of the ionosphere can produce an error from as little as a few feet to as much as 200 feet (60 meters). It tends to be worse at dawn and dusk, when the ionosphere is most active, and best at night, when things quiet down. All GPS receivers have a built-in prediction for ionospheric conditions that reduces the error to roughly 30 feet (10 meters); this can be improved considerably, as you'll see in the next section.

The geometry of the satellites also plays a major role in accuracy. The ideal configuration is several satellites spread above the horizon and one satellite directly overhead. But as the angles between satellites decrease, so does the accuracy of your position (often referred to as Dilution of Precision [DOP]).

Most handheld GPS units take satellite geometry into account and give an estimation of position error. If you walk from an open area toward a large object, such as a building, you can watch the accuracy rapidly decrease—perhaps going from 25 to 200 feet (7 to 60 meters)—as more of the sky is blocked. You are still getting a position reading from the remaining satellites in view, but the angles are suboptimal.

Another source of error can occur when you're near tall objects, such as cliffs and buildings, that can reflect the signal toward you. Termed *multipath error*, the bouncing signal can confuse the GPS receiver slightly.

For the first seventeen years of operation, the GPS signal available to the public was purposely degraded by the Department of Defense so that enemies could not use it. A process known as *Selective Availability* deliberately made the signal fuzzy so that a receiver was only accurate to about 330 feet (100 meters). However, workarounds were developed that made this practice obsolete, so Selective Availability was permanently turned off on May 2, 2000.

Adding up all of these variables, a standard handheld GPS receiver can place you within a 50-foot (15-meter) circle anywhere on the planet with a clear view of the sky. Often, a GPS receiver is accurate to half that area or less. And for most outdoor applications, that's certainly good enough.

Greater Accuracy

When necessary, such as when you're trying to locate an equipment cache, there are a number of methods to increase the accuracy of standard GPS receivers.

An artificial "satellite" can be established at a precisely determined position. This base station receives the signal, corrects for any errors, then broadcasts a corrected signal over anywhere from 2 to 200 miles (3 to 330 kilometers). Used by the Coast Guard along the coasts and major waterways to control shipping, "differential GPS" can be very accurate (to within inches) depending upon equipment and distance from the base station.

While effective, differential GPS functions only within a limited range and loses accuracy the farther away you get. It's great for surveyors but of limited value for most recreational users.

For better air traffic control, the Federal Aviation Administration has developed the Wide Area Augmentation System (WAAS), which is basically differential GPS on a nationwide scale. The system was commissioned on July 10, 2003, and continues to evolve.

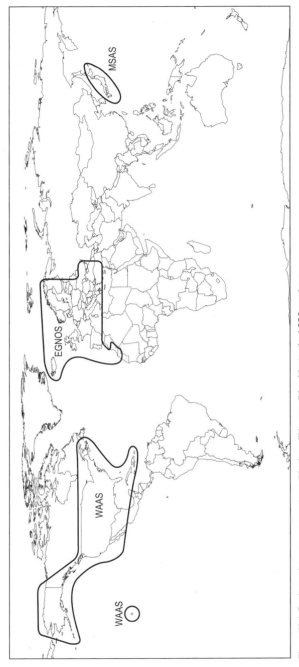

Figure 10.4 Regions where more accurate positioning will be possible with standard GPS receivers.

A similar GPS augmentation system, called the Euro Geostationary Navigation Overlay Service (EGNOS), is just coming online over Europe. And the Japanese Multi-Functional Satellite Augmentation System (MSAS) should be operational in 2006 (see Figure 10.4). More are planned for India, China, South Africa, and other regions.

In the United States, WAAS currently uses twenty-five ground stations around the country to collect GPS data and correct for ionospheric and system errors.

The information is relayed to master stations and sent to two satellites in geosynchronous orbit near the equator over 22,000 miles (35,000 kilometers) high; one is roughly over Brazil and the other above Hawaii. These will be replaced in the next few years with more sophisticated versions in different locations.

If your receiver is WAAS-enabled and can see any of the geosynchronous satellites, your position accuracy can improve to 10 feet (3 meters). It will also give you that level of accuracy in most of Europe and a good portion of Asia since EGNOS and MSAS use the same correction signals.

As with differential GPS, the farther you are from a ground station, the less accurate the correction. In some cases, leaving WAAS on can actually increase position error.

Because there are so few satellites and they don't move, the WAAS signal is rather easily blocked by your body or another object. Of course, this isn't a problem for airplanes.

For recreational use, WAAS is seldom needed. This is discussed further in Chapter 11.

Choosing a GPS

When considering the purchase of a handheld GPS unit, first determine your needs and budget. These days, even the most basic $100 GPS unit can locate your position to within 25 feet and is more than adequate for augmenting your map and compass. The question is: how many extra bells and whistles do you need?

Even if price isn't an issue, more features aren't always better. They often come with greater power requirements, so batteries drain even faster—already a weak point with all GPS units. Fancier models tend to be heavier and bulkier. And their greater complexity means you may want to factor in the extra weight of carrying the manual too.

While early GPS units were one-type-fits-all, the newer models are designed for specific applications. In general, a receiver intended for use in the outdoors does a poor job of navigating city streets: the screens are too small, there are no (or inadequate) driving directions, and they can be dangerous to operate while hurtling down the highway.

If you really want a driving computer, select an automobile GPS receiver (hardwired to the car) or a model designed to attach to a notebook or handheld computer (some GPS receivers don't even have a screen or controls). There are now even cell phones that offer route-finding capabilities and are well suited to getting around town.

For use in the backcountry, however, you want a lightweight, durable model with a reasonable battery life. Compactness, ease of operation if you wear gloves, and performance in low temperatures may be other considerations (see Figures 10.5 through 10.7).

All of the modern GPS units suitable for the back-country have at least twelve receiving channels, each of which tracks a satellite (called a *parallel design*). Their sophisticated electronics and software make these far superior to the early GPS receivers that tracked only eight or fewer satellites.

For the sake of comparison, the standard-issue military GPS units—properly known as Precision Lightweight GPS Receivers (PLGRs, often called "plug-gers")—weigh in at 2.75 pounds (1.25 kg). Nearly 200,000 of these bricks have been issued and, though more accurate than civilian models, they are primitive by current standards. The next-generation units—called Defense Advanced GPS Receivers (DAGRs, or "daggers")—will weigh less than a pound and include

Figure 10.5 The Suunto X9 (2.5 ounces, $700) offers GPS, altimeter, compass, and the usual watch features. Shown with the charging unit/computer interface.

mapping with aerial photos, a graphic interface, anti-jamming technology, and far greater accuracy (using both L1 and L2, while pluggers use only L1).

Following are some other features that may influence your purchase decision.

Water Resistance

Nearly all handheld GPS units are now designed to handle rain or even an accidental dip in the creek—in theory.

An IPX7 rating—the industry standard—indicates that the tested units still function after thirty minutes under 3 feet of water. (A rating of IPX4 means the device can handle only water splashes, while a rating of IPX8 indicates that it is designed for use underwater.)

Figure 10.6 The compact Garmin Gecko series (3.2 ounces, $95–$230) uses a pair of AAA batteries.

Figure 10.7 The Garmin eTrex series (5.5 ounces, $100–$400) runs from no frills to full-featured with mapping and color screens.

Unfortunately, *your* GPS receiver probably wasn't tested for water resistance before it left the factory. Even if it was, the rubber seals can harden and crack with age and usage. Don't bet your life on a single component that you can't see or test. If there's a significant chance of getting wet, use a Ziploc bag or two. And carry a backup compass and map.

Some GPS units are designed to float. If you spend a lot of time on or around the water, canoeing and kayaking, for instance, then this feature is worth having. Otherwise, when using a standard GPS unit on the occasional water trip, be sure to tie it in.

Antenna

There are two standard types of internal antennas used for handheld GPS units. The most common is known as a patch antenna; it is a small, flat square that is held parallel to the ground for best reception. The other style is the quadrifilar helix antenna, which resembles a tube that is pointed at the sky; the GPS is held vertically instead of horizontally.

For the most part, there is no practical difference in performance between a patch and a helix antenna. Both will receive the same signals under a clear sky and give equal accuracy. The helix has a slight advantage indoors because it "sees" closer to the horizon and so may pick up signals out a window better.

Although it is sometimes claimed that a helix antenna has better reception under tree cover, this is mostly a function of size. Smaller patch antennas are used in the tiniest GPS units, so they are less sensitive. But a GPS with a larger patch antenna can perform just as well as one with a helix antenna.

If sensitivity is needed under deciduous tree cover, you will want either a larger GPS unit or one that has a plug for an external amplified (not passive) antenna. In dense jungle, you may even need a telescoping pole to push the antenna higher up into the tree canopy. You will get better reception in the fall, when the leaves are dry, and winter, when leaves have fallen off.

Coniferous trees don't affect reception in the summer as much because the needles are so small. But in the winter, the trees hold more snow, which can affect reception.

Should you decide to compare the reception of different GPS units, remember that the test works only if performed at about the same time on the same day. Going back to a location on a different day means nothing since the satellites will be in different positions.

WAAS-Enabled

The ability to decipher the signal from WAAS and EGNOS satellites is increasingly becoming a standard feature. Since it is on the same frequency as the GPS satellites, no extra hardware is required. If a particular GPS unit has all the other features you need, the lack of WAAS should not dissuade you for most outdoor applications—you'll seldom need it and often can't get a signal anyhow.

Screen

Although most handheld GPS units have black-and-white or gray-scale screens, color screens are rapidly appearing and will eventually become the norm. For basic navigation purposes, four shades of gray are quite sufficient. But any GPS unit that offers maps will greatly benefit from a 256-color screen. And as technology continues to improve, power consumption and cost will continue to drop.

Whether the screen is gray scale or color, its size and resolution are also important. Larger screens (roughly 2¼ by 1½ inches) tend to offer easier viewing, particularly for older eyes that require reading glasses.

But a smaller screen (say 2 by 1 inches) with higher resolution (288 by 160 pixels instead of 240 by 160) can display more information. At the low end, a display might be only 100 by 64 pixels and that might suffice, since these units lack maps.

Perhaps the hardest viewing condition is under a cloudy but bright sky, since light is coming in from all angles. Direct sunlight can be trouble for some displays as well. Try to check viewability outdoors, not just in the store. If you wear polarized sunglasses, test the display while wearing them because some details may not be seen without rotating the display.

Also consider the effectiveness of the backlit display for use at dawn and dusk, as well as at night. Some are quite readable, while others can be seen only when held just right.

Power

Certainly the main bugaboo for GPS units in the field is their ravenous appetite for electricity. As a rule of thumb, look at the advertised battery life and cut it in half for planning trips. The lab tests make unrealistic assumptions about how the GPS unit will actually be used, though they are useful for comparing models within a brand (not against other company's products).

The smaller models accept only AAA batteries, so they are best fed with alkalines. Even though they are larger, receivers that take AA batteries give you the flexibility to use rechargeable NiMH batteries for local trips and readily available alkalines on longer excursions. If you will be using your GPS in a car, look for a model that can accept external power.

Maps

The latest innovation for handheld GPS units is the inclusion of "base maps" that cover an entire region or country. These include all the primary and secondary roads, towns and cities, and major terrain features such as lakes and rivers. Some models even have topographic information, but it is at a relatively small scale.

While sufficient for getting you to the trailhead, at present, none of the base maps are adequate for backcountry navigation. This can be partially remedied by installing more detail into the GPS, either with a chip or by downloading. This capability is available only on certain models and generally requires proprietary software. Some models now offer the same resolution as USGS topo maps (1:24,000); however, you are still limited by a small screen, so getting an overview of the terrain can take time.

At present, you cannot easily load maps from other programs onto a GPS unit. If you are computer savvy and have an abundance of free time, it is possible to create your own vector-based maps. While doing so is perhaps worthwhile for a specific area and need, most people will probably not find this practical.

When shopping for a GPS unit, remember that the base map is permanently built into the receiver—it cannot be replaced or changed. The GPS will still function if you go elsewhere and, if available, you can download maps for those areas. But it would be a mistake to purchase a GPS with a Europe base map if you live in the United States, or vice versa.

It bears repeating: No matter how fancy GPS units become, you should still carry a paper map and compass if you go into the backcountry! Relying on faint signals, breakable electronics, and fading batteries is risky.

Tracks and Routes

A "track" is essentially a string of electronic breadcrumbs laid down by the GPS unit as you travel. The individual dots have no name and can't be selected on their own. But, collectively, they show where you have been (when the unit was receiving). Tracks can fill up memory fast, so both more points (some can hold 10,000) and a control on the track rate are desirable.

When you mark a location with a GPS (or on the computer), you create a "waypoint." On a hike, you would create a waypoint at the trailhead, significant spots, and trail junctions. Connecting the waypoints creates a "route" that can be followed—the GPS almost pulls you along to the last waypoint.

For a 10-mile (16-kilometer) hike, you might use five to fifteen waypoints to describe a route, depending on the terrain. Most GPS units can store at least twenty routes with 125 waypoints each. And the deluxe models can hold fifty routes with 250 waypoints. Since most users will want to link their GPS unit and computer anyhow, the number of routes and waypoints stored isn't all that important.

Memory

As the above discussion implies, maps and tracks can fill up built-in memory in a hurry. As with computers, it's easy to have too little and almost impossible to have too much memory. If you will be uploading maps, look for at least 6 megabytes of internal memory.

Some models accept memory cards, which essentially frees you from constraints. You can preload maps onto the cards (from 8 to 128 megabytes) and easily swap them for visits to different areas. This is more convenient than downloading the data from a computer every time you travel.

Computer Interface

Much of the real advantage of GPS comes from the ability to connect the receiver to a computer running mapping software. The resulting synergy gives you the most powerful navigation tools available. Another advantage of a computer interface is the ability to upgrade firmware on the GPS unit; sometimes features are added or bugs are fixed.

So far, GPS manufacturers have been slow to switch from old-fashioned serial cables to much faster USB connections. Given the choice, a direct USB connection (without an adapter) is the way to go.

Altimeter

Due to poor satellite geometry in many locations, GPS units may not always provide an accurate altitude.

Even under ideal conditions, the vertical accuracy will seldom be better than 200 percent of horizontal (if the receiver claims your position is accurate to 20 feet, then vertical height is accurate to 40 feet).

Some GPS models have a built-in sensor that can provide a better estimation of your height above sea level. These offer all the same advantages and limitations of altimeters pointed out in Chapter 9. However, unlike a standard altimeter, a few receivers can use satellite data to calibrate the altitude, thus correcting for changes in the weather.

If you will be using your GPS in mountainous terrain, an altimeter function can be useful and doesn't add much (about $50) to the cost. On the other hand, if you will mostly be in the flatlands or sticking to roads, this is an option you can easily live without.

Although GPS altimeters can also display barometric trends, you must leave the unit turned on the entire time, so be sure you have an abundance of batteries.

Compass

Usually the models with an altimeter also come with a built-in electronic compass. This can be a handy features for hikers and skiers because a standard GPS (sans compass) cannot display direction when you are standing still or moving slowly. Models with a compass also make it easier to locate the satellites overhead so you can move accordingly to unblock a signal.

While convenient, a built-in compass has several drawbacks. Every time you change the batteries, you must recalibrate the compass, a procedure that takes a couple of minutes. And you'll be changing the batteries often since the compass can cut battery life almost in half. A simple alternative is to purchase a zipper-pull compass and attach it to your jacket or pack.

If you want this feature, look for a model that allows the compass to be turned on and off with the push of a button instead of by commands buried within menus. Most electronic compasses require the unit to be held level, sometimes tricky when there is no bubble level. The nicer 3-D electronic compasses provide an accurate reading no matter in which position the GPS unit is held.

Automobile Features

Although a GPS unit designed for the outdoors is less than ideal in a car, they can still be serviceable for that task. If you anticipate driving around with your GPS on a regular basis, you may wish to consider a model with a feature called *rubber banding*, which makes the route stay with the road.

This allows you to set a route between two points and have the GPS point in the proper direction as you are driving. Without rubber banding, as a curvy road veers away from the next waypoint, the direction arrow will not point down the road. This feature requires downloading the appropriate street maps onto the GPS. Rubber banding will not work with trails or even bike paths, so it's strictly a car thing.

Geocache

As this game of electronic hide-and-seek grows in popularity, some GPS units now have features that simplify the process. This can help you locate the cache, provide hints (if supplied by the cacher), and log the find. There are even games to play that can help familiarize you with GPS functions.

Future of GPS

Global positioning systems are here to stay. There is no way that the Department of Defense will ever prohibit the GPS system to civilians. Likewise, it will never restore Selective Availability. In the past decade, GPS has become a vital part of worldwide commerce and traffic control.

Indeed, GPS receivers will become even more accurate as new satellites are launched and technology improves. Much of the driving force for GPS growth is improved air traffic control that will allow "free flight," going directly between cities instead of following traffic lanes.

GPS is now essential for shipping, mining, farming, earth moving, surveying, mapping, and scientific work such as wetlands management, geological fault monitoring, and wildlife tracking.

Within the next few years, most cell phones will transmit their coordinates so that rescue personnel can quickly locate callers. We are also likely to see digital cameras that record the location from which each photo was taken.

When the European Galileo system comes online in 2008, adventurers will be able to broadcast an emergency signal to the satellites. Similar to the existing system of EPIRBs (Emergency Position Indicating Radio Beacons), which broadcasts at 406 megahertz, the new system will be faster and also send a return signal to indicate that help is on the way.

Currently, Block IIR-M satellites are being launched to replace older space vehicles as they reach the end of their life. This third-generation constellation will be fully operational by 2007. These satellites add a second civilian frequency (L2), which will help correct for atmospheric conditions.

Not far behind will be Block IIF satellites, which will begin launching in 2005 and should be fully running by 2011 or so. These will have a third civilian frequency (L5) for air traffic control.

Beyond that, plans are already in the works for Block III, which will be a major overhaul of the GPS system. The constellation will be reduced from six to three orbital planes, and other upgrades are expected. The system won't be ready until around 2015.

11.

Using Your GPS

Stop! Do not pass Go. If you've skipped ahead to this
chapter, go back to Chapter 7, "Using Your Compass":
read, mark, learn, and inwardly digest. Heading into
the field with a GPS unit but no background knowledge is a recipe for disaster. Quite simply, you're up the
creek without a paddle if you can't find your way home
when your electronic gadget malfunctions.

The wise backcountry traveler always brings a
backup map and compass to accompany the GPS unit.
Aside from simply running out of battery power, even
the best electronics can fail if dropped onto a rock.
Sure, they are tough and can withstand most abuse.
But it's that one time in ten thousand, when either you
or machine screws up, that can leave you stranded in a
bad situation.

At Home

If you want to protect your investment, the first thing
you should do is go to an office supply store and purchase a package of PDA screen protectors. These are
clear plastic sheets with adhesive on the back that can
be trimmed to fit the exact dimensions of the LCD on
your GPS unit. Covering the screen will prevent the
otherwise inevitable scratches on the soft plastic that
can eventually make the GPS hard to read.

You might also consider attaching a lanyard to your GPS unit to reduce the chance of an accidental drop. A 6-inch loop of cord is sufficient to slip a hand through but not so long that it tangles with everything.

When you purchase a new GPS unit, it's a good idea to purchase extra batteries right away or make sure you have topped off your rechargeables. You will burn through the provided alkaline batteries in no time and there is a lot to learn.

Presets

After you power up your GPS unit for the first time, navigate to the settings screen (called "Setup" by Garmin and Lowrance, "Preferences" by Magellan, and "Units" by Suunto). Here you will change the factory presets, since they are probably incorrect for most trail users.

Map Datum. Before you can accurately use a GPS unit, you must be certain it is speaking the same lingo as your paper maps, that is, that you are using the same map datum and coordinate system. Most receivers will come from the factory set to the 1984 World Geodetic System (WGS 84) map datum, since that is what GPS is based upon.

As you'll recall from Chapter 2, most of the topographic maps in the United States and Canada are based upon the 1927 North American datum (NAD 27). Depending upon your location, the coordinates generated by a GPS unit set to WGS 84 can be off by more than 600 feet from a map made with NAD 27.

Conversely, if you are using nautical or aerial charts, be sure to switch the GPS unit back to WGS 84 (or NAD 83, which is the same) since they are based on that datum. When traveling outside North America, you will need to check which map datum is used (there are nearly two hundred worldwide) and change accordingly.

If you are using digital maps, the software can switch to the datum you prefer. Most use WGS 84 as a default, which is fine as long as your GPS is also set accordingly. Just be aware that errors can arise if you are also using USGS-printed topos, so it may make sense to set everything to NAD 27.

Map Grid. Most GPS units are also preset to use the standard latitude/longitude grid system. While this may be more familiar to many people, as explained in Chapter 3, the UTM (Universal Transverse Mercator) system is even easier once you get used to it. The sooner you switch your GPS unit to UTM (typically on the same settings page as map datum), the sooner you can take advantage of this system.

If you will be traveling in the Arctic or Antarctic, you will use the Universal Polar Stereographic (UPS) grid. In the United Kingdom, many maps use the Ordinance Survey of Great Britain, so set your GPS unit to the OSGB grid.

Battery Mode. Although many GPS units have a "battery saver" function, it can create more problems than it solves. When the battery saver is turned on, instead of taking a fix every second, the GPS unit checks its position every five seconds and it only looks for satellites well above the horizon. This mode can reduce battery consumption by about 30 percent.

However, the battery saver mode is a nuisance in areas with a weak signal, such as a forest or the bottom of a canyon. When it switches off, the GPS unit loses its lock on satellites and must reacquire the signal. Unless you routinely travel in wide-open spaces, it's better to turn off battery saver.

Many GPS units now have an option for setting the type of battery used (alkaline, NiCad, NiMH, lithium). When this option is set, it provides a more accurate estimation of remaining battery life.

Satellite View. As explained in Chapter 10, your GPS unit works on "line of sight" with satellites that transmit very weak signals. In practice, this means that GPS has a difficult time in many locations and doesn't work at all in some places.

For best accuracy, your GPS unit needs to show you where the satellites are and their signal strength. However, some models hide this valuable information in an "Advanced Skyview" setting (see Figure 11.1).

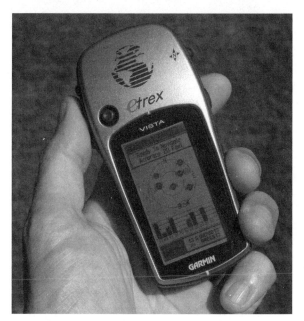

Figure 11.1 Satellite view screen.

Don't be intimidated by this nomenclature; switch to the "Advanced Skyview" setting from "Normal" to get the most out of your receiver. Using the graphic image of satellite locations, you can change your location for a better signal, hence a more accurate position fix.

WAAS. If you are in the contiguous United States, Alaska, and parts of Canada, you can turn on WAAS (Wide Area Augmentation System) reception for maximum accuracy (10 feet, 3 meters). But in a lot of areas, it won't do any good, and it has a few drawbacks besides.

WAAS was developed for aircraft and is seldom available on the ground. Though it is widely hyped by GPS receiver manufacturers, in practice, it seldom achieves the promised accuracy (details below).

Outside the United States, trying to use WAAS can actually throw you further off course. If you are far from a ground station that provides correction data for the atmosphere, the satellite signal can give you erroneous information.

Declination. If your GPS unit has a built-in compass, it will give you the option of manually setting the declination. Some will even do this automatically, but you would be wise to verify that it agrees with your maps (unless they are old; see Chapter 8).

Altimeter Calibration. As with any other altimeter, if your GPS unit has this function, you must manually enter a known altitude to get accurate readings. Fortunately, the GPS unit makes it easy to determine your position on a map and thus to read the correct altitude.

A few GPS units have the option of automatic calibration, which uses satellite data to compensate for changing weather conditions. (The altitude may be off considerably when you first turn on the GPS unit but will normalize with time if you have a good three-dimensional fix.)

Units. Make sure the measures of speed, distance, time, temperature, and barometric pressure are set up the way you like them. These units can be changed at any time, but it's best to start with familiar settings. If you're using the UTM grid, it can be more convenient to measure distance in meters, although it isn't absolutely necessary.

Sound. Turn it off. Some GPS units offer a variety of alarms to tell you if you are off course or near your destination. Aside from being obnoxious for those around you, they really aren't necessary.

Lasting Power

The Achilles heel of any GPS unit is its need for power; these things suck batteries the way a Hummer sucks gasoline. The simple solution is to carry more batteries. But this isn't always practical on longer trips since the weight and bulk can be prohibitive. And sometimes stopping to replace batteries is a considerable nuisance (e.g., it can't be done while wearing gloves). Thus, conserving energy is often the best solution.

As discussed earlier, turning on "Battery Saver" can be a poor solution, because you will frequently lose signals—increasing battery life doesn't do much good if you still don't know where you are.

For most GPS units that have them, electronic compasses increase battery drain by about 40 percent (the Brunton Atlas MNS is an exception). Another significant drain comes from the backlight. While these features can be handy, minimize usage to prolong battery life.

Unless you need a detailed track log showing every step of your journey, there is little reason to leave the GPS unit turned on when you hike. As long as you started out the excursion with a good position fix and the GPS unit is stowed in a convenient pocket, it takes only thirty to forty-five seconds to power up and find your position. One annoyance with turning off and on the GPS unit is the long delay of start-up screens that do little more than advertise and offer a lawyer label (pointless disclaimer); sadly, this cannot be turned off, so time is wasted.

Given their voracious appetite for power, feeding GPS units with high-quality rechargeable batteries is a prudent move. Currently, the best option is nickel metal hydride (NiMH) batteries combined with a "smart" charger that most effectively tops them off. Look for a minimum storage capacity of 2,000 mAh (milliampere-hours) in AA batteries; some batteries now hold 2,500 mAh. In comparison, good alkaline batteries hold about 2,800 mAh of juice, though they don't discharge as fast during storage.

Compass Quirks

While gadgetitis may lure you into spending extra for a GPS unit with a built-in compass (standard with a built-in altimeter, although unrelated), this option does come with some notable quirks. First, it doesn't replace anything in your pack—contrary to marketing hype. On any trip where the route home is not blindingly obvious, you must still carry a backup magnetic compass (preferably one with a baseplate, so you can work with paper maps).

The reason for an electronic compass is to provide directions when you are standing still or walking slowly, something a GPS unit alone cannot do (it only tracks position and cannot tell where you are looking). However, the direction the compass indicates is magnetic North will be off considerably (20° or more) unless it is properly calibrated.

This means that *every* time the batteries are changed, you must go through a 2-minute calibration process before using the compass. Some GPS units will remind you after a battery switch, while others assume you will remember and can navigate through the menus to find the calibration feature.

Most electronic compasses must be held level for an accurate reading. Unfortunately, they are also fairly sensitive to slight changes and often don't provide good visual clues such as a bubble level; they can be tough to use while on the go. If you consider an electronic compass an important feature, look for a GPS unit that offers a three-axis design so it reads correctly when held at any angle.

WAAS

Ah, the catalog copy reads fantastic . . . know your position within 10 feet. Sounds great. But if you read the microprint, you'll find that WAAS isn't all that useful for most outdoor users.

The main problem is you'll seldom get a signal from either of the two satellites currently providing WAAS. The SV (space vehicle) known as AOR-W (Atlantic Ocean Region West) is in a stationary orbit over Brazil and its counterpart, POR (Pacific Ocean Region), is sort of south of Hawaii. Both of these are about 10,000 miles higher than GPS satellites, but they are near the equator and do not move.

These satellites work well for airplanes and ships, since a clear line of sight is always possible. But the WAAS satellites are easily obscured by land features. And the farther north you go, the lower the WAAS satellites sit on the horizon.

On most GPS receivers, AOR-W is designated number 35 and POR is number 47. Over Europe, AOR-E is designated number 33, and Asia is covered by IOR number 44, although these are not operational at this time. More WAAS satellites will be added in the future, so positions and numbers may change but will always be greater than 32.

If you can get a lock on a WAAS satellite, it takes about five minutes to download the necessary information. This includes all the information from two dozen ground stations around North America to correct for ionospheric changes. When enough information is available, the Garmin screen shows a *D* next to each satellite that has differential correction. But this increase in accuracy lasts only about two minutes when the WAAS signal is blocked.

When you have a full differential lock using WAAS, the accuracy of the GPS unit doubles (from about 18 feet to 9 feet). But it takes a fair amount of effort to narrow your search that little bit. It may be handy for some applications, but most of the time you just don't need to bother.

If you turn off WAAS reception, you'll get faster fixes on your position, maps will draw faster, and battery drain decreases.

Navigating by GPS

A GPS receiver, no matter how basic or fancy, tells you three things: where you are, where you've been, and the direction of where you want to go (if it's been told). The deluxe models embellish these basics with niceties—often at the cost of complexity.

Unfortunately, poorly written GPS unit manuals seem to be the norm rather than the exception. Nonetheless, you really need to read the manual to learn the details of your chosen model. Although they share much in common, the specifics vary widely between manufacturers and even within a model series.

This section attempts to clear the air about the standard GPS unit features and operation.

Sky View

It's such an important concept to using GPS that it needs reiterating: the "quality" of the view of the sky directly affects accuracy of your position. The more obstructions—be they canyon walls, trees, or even your own body—the harder it becomes to get a good fix.

Even if your receiver shows that you have strong signals from four satellites, their geometry relative to where you are standing is important. If all the "visible" satellites are clustered directly above you, the estimated position will not be very accurate, especially in the vertical component.

Thus, whenever you pull out your GPS unit, you need to be thinking about what is overhead.

The most accurate fixes will be found in a big, open field or on top of a peak where you have unobstructed views to the horizon. In other situations, you need to pay attention to the satellite view screen to see which satellites are blocked. Many times, just moving a couple of feet or turning your body will improve signals.

Before you head into a forest, it helps to stop at a clearing and get a strong signal from as many satellites as possible. The GPS unit has a much easier time keeping a lock on a satellite than acquiring it, so you'll maintain a better sense of location. Try to stop at least once an hour to get a lock on new satellites that have moved into view.

The type of forest you are in and the time of year also make a difference. Among deciduous trees, the signals will deteriorate in the spring and summer, when broad leaves have a lot of water content and can reflect signals. Meanwhile, coniferous forests tend to block signals more in the winter when snow covers branches.

Start-Up

When you fire up a GPS unit for the first time, it may take five to fifteen minutes to achieve a fix. This also applies if it has been off for a few months or if you've moved several hundred miles from its last position.

Before it can tell you where you are, the GPS unit must first download an almanac that contains the rough position of all of the satellites (the SVs transmit the almanac). It also must download the ephemeris (the precise location data) from each of the satellites within its current view.

When the almanac is outdated or invalidated by a big move, the GPS unit starts from scratch; some models allow (or force) you to enter the approximate time and position to help speed the process. The almanac information is good for a couple months, so you don't have to go through this process very often.

The ephemeris data is good only for a few hours. When this information is outdated, the GPS unit must go through a "cold start" that takes one to two minutes. So don't be surprised if your GPS unit is a bit slow waking up in the morning.

After the current ephemeris has been downloaded, turning on the GPS unit is called a "warm start" and you should get a position fix in about fifteen seconds.

Waypoints

There are two basic methods for using waypoints: mark them in the field as you go, or preinstall them before your trip. The first method is used to get you back to your starting point and to help return to a location at a later date. Whey you install waypoints ahead of time, you can use the GPS unit to "pull" you to the destination.

Creating a waypoint or Point of Interest (POI; a location that isn't part of a route) in the field is easy if you have a position fix: just press the appropriate button. This opens a new screen that allows you to name the waypoint (see Figure 11.2). Since this is usually a tedious process due to the lack of a keyboard (lots of scrolling for each letter), it is often better to use the sequentially numbered defaults for marking a trail.

When you get home, assuming you have the technology, you can upload the waypoints to your computer and rename them at your leisure. However, if you must

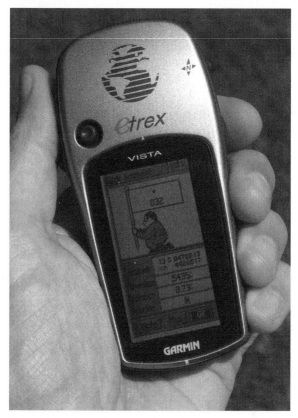

Figure 11.2 Marking a waypoint.

return to a particular location during a trip, and an autogenerated number like *012* is too cryptic to remember what it represents, it's worth taking the time to rename it "Camp" or "Cache" so there is no confusion.

Returning to a waypoint can be as easy as selecting it from a menu and pressing the "GoTo" command. This switches you to a Navigation screen with a pointer (or virtual road) that directs you to the waypoint. If you get off course, the navigation screen helps bring you back to the proper heading. It also indicates how far away you are and even the (very rough) estimated time of arrival. Although the pointer may resemble a compass, it's important to remember that this needle does not point North but rather points to the designated waypoint.

Some GPS units offer a Man Overboard (MOB) function. When you hit the panic buttons, the device automatically marks the spot and puts itself into a navigation mode that brings you back. This is a worthwhile feature for those who spend time on water, although hopefully you'll never need it.

Routes

When you string together a series of waypoints, you create a "route." While just using a single waypoint will eventually get you there, it doesn't show the best course taking into account trails and obstacles.

The optimal way to use routes is to preprogram the GPS unit while you're at home using mapping software on the computer. Trying to do this manually on the GPS unit is just asking for trouble–it's way too easy to transpose numbers when entering coordinates, a mistake that can put you far off course. If the GPS unit has built-in topo maps, creating a route manually is more feasible; however, it's still easier on a computer with a large screen and more power.

As a general rule, it takes about ten to fifteen waypoints to adequately plot out a 10-mile hike. If the terrain is convoluted with lots of side trails, you may need to double the number of waypoints. Open terrain with just a few intersections may require a waypoint only every now and then.

Following a route is just a matter of going from waypoint to waypoint. When you reach a waypoint, the GPS unit will provide a bearing and distance to the next one. You can either use the navigation screen and just follow the pointer or switch to the mapping screen to see where you are relative to other waypoints (and terrain features if the GPS unit offers topo maps).

It's also a simple matter to reverse course on a route. You essentially tell the GPS unit "I wanna go home" with the push of a few buttons, and it will provide reverse bearings.

Tracks

If you leave your GPS unit turned on while wandering about, it will automatically store a history of where you've been. Called a *track* on most receivers (some use the term *plot trail*), it's rather like the crumbs left by Hansel and Gretel without pesky birds to gobble them, rain to wash them away, or snow to hide them.

The track feature is generally automatic, marking the path at its own discretion, and it does a reasonable job. Some GPS units also allow you to customize the recording units so you can specify the distance or time intervals used. If you will be turning the GPS unit off between position fixes, there is no reason to create a track log; it just creates clutter and takes up memory.

A track log may contain a few hundred to many thousands of entries (the limit depends on the memory capacity of the GPS unit). Although these log entries contain time and location information, unlike with waypoints, you usually cannot edit this information.

When you reach your turnaround point, you can save the track and then use it to retrace your steps.

Back home, you can upload the track to your computer's mapping software to get a full analysis of your excursion. This is a particularly useful feature for search-and-rescue teams to see what areas have been covered. The software can also convert a track to a route for return visits.

If you will be relying on the tracking feature, it's important to position your GPS unit so that it constantly receives a signal as you are moving. This may require carrying the GPS attached to a shoulder strap or in a pack pocket so that the antenna is properly oriented (horizontal for patch antennas, vertical for quad helix).

GPS Games

While orienteering is a race-oriented navigation sport, geocaching is more of a family-oriented recreation. Instead of racing from control point to control point using map and compass, geocachers meander to their UTM coordinates with a GPS unit pointing the way.

The caches are scattered all over the planet, from city parks to remote locations. Clues and ratings of terrain difficulty are provided, so you can choose a cache that suits you. When you find a cache, typically a waterproof container, you are supposed to take something, leave something, and leave a message in the logbook. People leave all sorts of things, from books to jewelry, foreign coins to music CDs.

All of this is organized through the website www.geocaching.com—just enter your zip code for a list of caches in your area. You'll find updates here on geocaching regulations made by parks and land management agencies to protect lands and wildlife. There are also local clubs of cache hunting enthusiasts.

For those who need competition, there is geodashing (http://geodashing.gpsgames.org). A computer randomly picks a large number of points all over the planet. Then the race is on to reach as many as possible before the deadline. Dashers compete solo or in teams, and there is no advantage to living in a particular place. The first team to a dashpoint gets three points, the second team two points, and the rest one point.

Yet another GPS activity is called the Degree Confluence Project (http://confluence.org). The goal is to visit the meeting point of lines of latitude and longitude, then photograph the location and send in a report.

There are 14,027 confluences that can be reached on land (called a primary confluence), literally all over the world. At present, fewer than 3,500 have been successfully documented, though 155 countries are represented. The closest confluence is less than 50 miles (80 kilometers) from you now, unless you are reading this on a plane or a ship.

Computer Networking

Connecting your GPS receiver to a computer gives you the full benefit of modern navigation technology. How much you can take advantage of this depends upon your hardware and software.

Hooking Up

While the makers of handheld GPS receivers have done a fabulous job of designing and building their products, they have paid less attention to making their products fully compatible with computers. What should be a simple, intuitive process is often tedious and at times frustrating.

Currently, many of the GPS units use an old-fashioned serial connection; this usually requires a $50 adapter since most newer computers have only USB ports. While a serial connection is adequate for simple transfers of waypoints and routes, it is painfully slow for exchanging maps.

Newer GPS units are starting to switch over to USB connections, which are much faster. However, software compatibility and lack of drivers are presently an issue. Even more promising is the use of Bluetooth wireless technology so that no cables are needed to exchange data.

Many companies offer their own software, for a fee of course, yet it's clear that a good user interface is not their forte. This is often required to take advantage of all the features of a higher-end GPS unit, though you may still end up buying other mapping software too.

One very weak point with GPS units and mapping software is poor support for Macintosh computers, despite their popularity among outdoor enthusiasts (about one-quarter of market share by one estimate). Mac users can get by with running the Windows software in Virtual PC, but it's a poor solution with zero technical support and requires dealing with an ungainly interface.

Mapping Software

If you just want to transfer waypoints to and from your GPS unit, there are a number of inexpensive (even free) mapless programs available for this task. These are ideal for inputting waypoints by keyboard instead of entering them manually on the receiver. However, this basic software does little else, so it really doesn't tap into the capabilities of the technology.

In Chapter 2, we discussed the many advantages of using digital mapping software. The ability to plot out trips ahead of time and create custom maps is very handy. Using such software in conjunction with a GPS unit yields an even more powerful navigation system.

In general, there are three types of mapping software: proprietary, commercial topographic, and commercial importing programs.

All of the GPS units that have mapping capability come with a base map of the United States (or Europe) that shows major roads and cities. However, these do not include topographic information, or information at street-level detail. If you want this information stored in your GPS, you will need to purchase additional software.

Using proprietary software from the GPS unit manufacturers is the easiest way to upload detailed road and topographic maps. Each company uses its own data format, so you are dependent upon them to provide maps for your GPS unit. Each major brand (Brunton, Garmin, Lowrance, and Magellan) offers its own database as an option.

For the most part, none of the GPS units can use scanned maps, software maps from other suppliers, or USGS digital raster graphic (DRG) maps. (If you are very tech-savvy, you can create vector maps and upload them, but it's a complex, time-consuming procedure.)

In general, the commercial programs with topographic maps on CD or DVD are more sophisticated than what the GPS companies offer. Some major brands include Delorme Topo USA, Maptech Terrain Navigator and Terrain Navigator Pro (the Mercedes of consumer software), Memory-Map Navigator, and National Geographic Topo. These offer features such as shaded relief,

3-D views, and aerial photo overlays and usually have a better user interface (see Figure 11.3).

Although you cannot upload these maps directly to a GPS unit, you can still carry them with you if you own a Pocket PC. Several mapping programs can transfer maps from your main computer to these handhelds. However, none of the Pocket PCs are nearly as rugged or water resistant as a GPS unit, so great care must be taken to protect them in the field.

When none of the proprietary or third-party mapping programs offer digital maps for an area you are visiting, there is still another possibility: importing other maps. Some programs (such as Fugawi, MacGPS Pro, and OziExplorer) allow you to scan in a paper map and convert it to a digital format. Once the map has been imported, it can be used with your GPS unit to exchange track and route information.

Transferring Data

All of these mapping programs can connect directly with most GPS receivers to download tracks and upload routes and points of interest.

Before you head out on a trip, you can plot out your course by creating waypoints on the map and then connecting them into a route. Hook up your GPS unit and download all of the information. Then print out paper maps for the area and you are ready to navigate.

Out in the field, you can add waypoints—perhaps to mark an important trail junction, a great vista, or a good fishing spot—then upload them back home. You will have a permanent record that you can edit with notes, and even include photos, for your next visit.

If you leave the GPS unit on while you are traveling, it will create a track that you can save to keep a record of where you've been. Once the track is uploaded onto your computer, you can analyze your movements in far more detail than that provided by the GPS unit. The software can also convert the track into a route so you can follow the same path (routes use up much less memory than tracks).

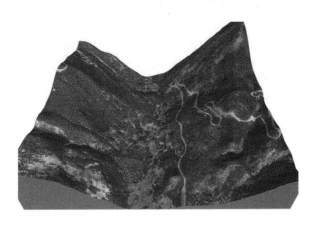

Figure 11.3 Three views of Trail Ridge Road (compare with the foldout map) created with Maptech Terrain Navigator Pro. The flat topo map was rendered in 3-D and overlaid with aerial photos.

Some of the programs even offer moving maps for use while driving. By connecting the GPS unit to a laptop or handheld computer, you can use the larger screen to see where you are in real time. However, a GPS unit designed for driving is a superior choice if you do this often.

12.

Direction
from the Sky

It is not often that a party finds itself without a compass. And compasses aren't likely to give up on you suddenly. Granted, you can drop a compass. Or you may have left it behind at last night's campsite. But it's not likely that all members of a party will lose their compasses, or leave them somewhere and not notice until hours away.

Unless you travel in a party of one.

You have been told not to by many experts. But some of us travel solo by necessity; none of our buddies can get away at the right time. Others solo by choice, balancing the rewards against the risks.

The soloist should always carry a spare compass.

So, if you have the tools, why bother with finding directions from the sky?

No book on land navigation would be complete without this information. Also, certain endlessly repeated methods for finding your way without a compass simply don't work, or work very poorly.

And perhaps the best reason of all, navigation by sun and stars can add to your fun. At the very least, it could be compared to learning about edible wild plants. After a nibble or two you can decide to stick to your freeze-dried diet.

So let's assume you find yourself without a compass or GPS unit. Where can you get directions?

Forget about the moss on the north side of trees. In some places it grows on all sides of the trunk, in others on none.

Trees may or may not betray the direction of the prevailing winds by their lean or growth. Not very good.

Eventually everybody comes up with the sun and the stars.

Popular but Inaccurate Methods

Unfortunately, there several oft-repeated techniques that sound plausible until you actually try them. These ignore a realm of truths that render your findings too inaccurate for navigation.

Finding South from the Sun and a Watch

The instructions for this method are deceptively simple. First, point the hour hand toward the sun. Some authors may suggest using a match or something similar to cast a shadow for aligning the hour hand with the sun. South is then halfway between the hour hand and twelve o'clock on your dial.

The logic behind this method sounds convincing. The earth turns on its axis—which makes the sun seem to travel through the sky—once in twenty-four hours. The sun is south at noon. And the hour hand turns once around the clock face in twelve hours. That's where the "halfway" instruction comes from.

The method works nicely near the North Pole in summer. It works fairly well in Alaska, northern Canada, and other lands in the same latitudes.

In the northernmost parts of the contiguous United States it indicates within 7° from the true direction during the six winter months. In midsummer it's off as much as 23° either east or west of true South.

As you move southward, the error increases—to 24° in Key West (latitude 25°N) in the winter months, and to more than 70° in summer.

What was wrong with the logic? Nothing, except that it did not take into account that the sun in summer is high in the sky, whereas you hold your watch horizontally. Put differently, the sun's apparent movement does complete the twenty-fourth part of a full 360° circle around the earth in each hour, or 15° per hour. But the sun's bearing, measured on the horizon with a compass, is far from that. For example, in midsummer in Key West the sun changes a mere 5° between 6 and 7 A.M. (all times local mean time). Between 11 A.M. and noon it changes bearing 86°.

You may think Key West is just too far south for this method. But halfway between the southern and northern limits of the contiguous United States, at latitude 37°N, the summer error still reaches an intolerable 32°.

You'd have to go to the Brooks Range of Alaska, north of the Arctic Circle, to get the error down to about 10° in summer. In winter the maximum error there is down to 3°.

All these figures assume that you align the hour hand exactly with the sun, say by the shadow method. They also assume that you have allowed for daylight saving time by subtracting one hour when it's in effect. They further assume that you have corrected for the difference in longitude between your position and your standard time meridian, and that you have made yet another correction—for the time of noon itself—about which you'll read presently. These last corrections can easily amount to another three-quarters of an hour.

Making all these corrections yields accurate results within 7° between latitudes 37°N and 49°N during the cool six months of the year!

Finding East from the Motion of a Stick's Shadow

Another method you may have heard or read about makes use of the shadow that the tip of a vertical object casts on the ground.

The logic sounds unimpeachable: since the sun seems to move from east to west, the shadow must move from west to east.

Plant a stick, say four feet long—or a ski pole, tip up in the snow—and mark the point where the tip's shadow falls now; wait about fifteen minutes and again mark the point where the shadow falls.

A line connecting these points will run west-east, the second point being the more easterly.

The method sounds appealing since it requires no watch. You could just take a good rest until the shadow has moved far enough to tell in what direction it's moving.

Since time is not involved, you don't have to use any of the corrections that the watch method entails. And East and West, of course, are just as good directions as North or South for finding all other directions.

There might be difficulties at some locations finding a soft spot in which to erect your 4-foot shadow pole. The vertical is no great problem; you could improvise a plumb line from a fishing line, dental floss, or whatever. The real problem is the area on which the shadow is to fall. It must be level and horizontal.

But even when it's used on level ground, this method is not as logical as it sounds. While moving westward, the sun also rises (before noon) or drops (after noon). The method seems to imply that this movement doesn't amount to much in fifteen minutes.

The deviation from true East depends on your latitude, the date, and the time of day. Nowhere in the latitude of the contiguous United States can you get consistent results with errors of less than 20° or 30°.

Planting the pole so that at first it does not cast a shadow at all—that is, facing the sun—does not improve the result. The moon's shadow is equally unsatisfactory, at times more so.

Recommended Methods

Now that you've seen the wrong ways, here are right ways to find directions without a compass. The first method is more practical at sea, since there aren't many places on land where you have an unobstructed, level horizon.

The Bearing of the Sun at Sunrise and Sunset

This method requires no equipment whatsoever, just the sun. It is the method by which ships at sea have checked their compasses and determined compass error and variation (called declination ashore) for the past two centuries.

Using the nautical almanac for the year and a knowledge of his or her latitude, the navigator calculates the bearing of the sun at sunrise or sunset, accurate to one-tenth of 1°.

There are now many astronomy programs that can print charts showing time and location of sunrise and sunset for any given latitude. This information can also be found by searching the Internet (enter the term "sunrise calculator" in a search engine) and using the online programs. And it's a standard feature on many GPS receivers, although using this method with GPS is paradoxical.

Unlike the horizon at sea, the horizon on land almost everywhere is not a sharp horizontal line. The bearing of the rising or setting sun is calculated for the time when—at sea—the sun is about one-half of its diameter above the horizon.

It doesn't matter much how high you are when your horizon is at about the same level. Don't fret when you miss the actual sunrise or sunset by minutes, or when it takes place behind some low obstruction. Right after rising and just before setting the sun changes bearing rather slowly. For example, to change its bearing by a single degree takes it nine minutes at Key West (latitude 25°N), seven minutes in the middle of the contiguous United States (latitude 35°N), and five minutes in the north at latitude 54°N.

With a reasonably unobstructed horizon, it is unlikely that all the errors related to year, date, elevation, and your estimate of the actual horizon will result in a bearing that is off by more than 2°.

That may not be good enough to set the declination on your compass when better information is available to you. But it's certainly good enough to estimate

North or any other direction when you find yourself without a compass.

Finding South from the Bearing of the Sun at Noon

A slightly more accurate method for getting a bearing from the sun requires correct time—correct to the nearest half minute. If you set your watch properly before leaving on your trip, or you have a GPS receiver, you can use this method.

The principle of getting direction from the sun at noon is simple: in the Northern Hemisphere the sun at local noon bears exactly South, by definition. The opposite is true, of course, in the Southern Hemisphere; there, the sun would bear North.

The practical problem is to find the exact time of local apparent noon. Nothing else will do. The change of bearing of the sun is greatest at noon; that's why we have to be so accurate.

If the earth's orbit were a circle, and if the earth's axis were at right angles to the orbit, the sun would bear South every day at 12:00 noon local mean time (*mean* refers to the time that all clocks keep, based on a day that is exactly twenty-four hours long). The actual orbit is an ellipse, and the earth's axis is inclined about $23\frac{1}{2}°$ from the vertical. These two facts combine to make the sun bear South anywhere from one-quarter hour before to one-quarter hour after noon, local mean time.

The sun's actual time of bearing south, local apparent noon (sundial noon), is easily found online (e.g., www.solar-noon.com). Simply enter the longitude, latitude, and time zone to create a custom table.

There are good practical reasons for setting our watches to some form of standard time. When it's 12:00 noon local mean time in Washington, D.C., it's 12:40 P.M. in Eastport, Maine, and 11:44 A.M. in Savannah, Georgia. At one time, each of these cities actually operated on its own time. As a result, U.S. railroad timetables used at least fifty-six different times. That's no way to run railroads! Since November 18, 1883, the United States has operated on the four standard times we are still using.

Eastern Standard Time is the local mean time of any place at longitude 75°W. When it's local mean noon there, it's also noon in Washington, D.C., Eastport, and Savannah.

Theoretically, the Eastern Standard time zone extends 7½° of longitude east and west of the standard meridian, 75°W. That should leave out Eastport (67°W), which is just outside the eastern limit of that zone. But many small adjustments such as this have been made to avoid cutting through a town, a county, or a state.

With a few minor exceptions, the entire world operates on standard time meridians that are multiples of 15°; each zone in principle extends 7½° east and west and differs by exactly one hour from the next zone.

From the fact that the 15° zones differ by exactly one hour you can infer that for each degree of longitude the difference in local time would be exactly four minutes.

Eastport (longitude 67°W), 8° east of the standard meridian, is thirty-two minutes fast on Eastern Standard Time. Washington (longitude 77°W), 2° west of the standard meridian, is eight minutes slow on Eastern Standard Time. Savannah (longitude 81°W), 6° west of the standard meridian, is twenty-four minutes slow on Eastern Standard Time.

Put differently, local noon on April 15 falls at 12:00 noon at any place on the 75th meridian. On the same day, it falls at 11:28 A.M. in Eastport, 12:08 P.M. in Washington, D.C., and 12:24 P.M. in Savannah.

The four-minute-per-degree-longitude rule is not hard to remember. To decide where it's earlier and where it's later, just remember that the sun rises in the East and travels west. So it'll get to Eastport before it gets to the 75th meridian; and it'll get to that meridian before it gets to Washington, Savannah, and all points west of it.

If 1° causes a four-minute difference in time, then one-quarter degree (15′) will cause a one-minute difference.

To calculate your local time in standard time, first find your longitude—to the nearest quarter degree—from the top or bottom margin of the topo quad you are using. Compare that longitude with the longitude of the meridian of your standard time. In the United States, standard time meridians are as follows:

Eastern Standard Time 75°W
Central Standard Time 90°W
Mountain Standard Time 105°W
Pacific Standard Time 120°W

Say you are near Red Lodge, Montana, at longitude 109°20′, rounded to 109¼°. That's 4¼° west of your standard time meridian (105°). You can figure that four minutes times four makes sixteen minutes, plus one more for the quarter-degree makes seventeen minutes in all for the time difference.

You are west of the Mountain Standard Time meridian, so the sun gets to you seventeen minutes later.

The accuracy of the method is very good. The error of South (or North if down under the equator) found by a noon calendar is comparable in accuracy to that read from a baseplate compass corrected for declination.

Equal Altitude Method

You don't need accurate time, a table, or a knowledge of your longitude to use this method. Its only drawback is that it takes some time to wait for the result. It can be combined with a long lunch break.

The theory behind it is that the height of the sun above the horizon a given time *before* noon is virtually the same as it is for the same interval of time *after* noon, everywhere and at any date.

In practice, you measure the height by the length of the shadow. Before noon, you mark the shadow that the tip of some vertical object casts on a horizontal surface and measure the shadow's length from the base of

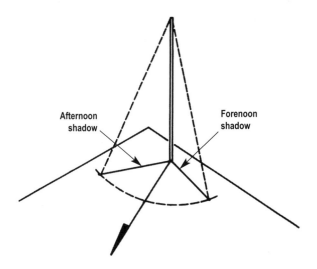

Figure 12.1 Equal altitude method for finding North from the sun.

the vertical object. When the shadow reaches that length again in the afternoon, you again mark it (see Figure 12.1).

A line from the center of the base of the object casting the shadow through the point halfway between your two marks points directly North.

The difficulties for the wilderness traveler are the vertical object and especially the horizontal plane. But if you take a lunch break at an organized campground, a pencil, a piece of string, and a picnic table will let you demonstrate the principle to anyone who wants to wait, watch, and check with a compass. So would a ski pole and a frozen-over lake, or a flagpole with a paved area to the north of it. Any error in the result is due to the crudeness of the tools, not the method.

Directions from the Sun: Tropics

The tropics are defined as the zone between 23½°N to 23½°S, approximately. They are also defined as the only zone on earth where the sun at noon can be directly overhead. Throughout the zone, that happens on two days of the year. (At the borders with the temperate zone the two days shrink to one.)

The sun and watch method, described above, and the shadow movement method are useless in tropical latitudes. The method based on the length of shadows before and after noon is valid, but during much of the year the shadow will be too short for accurate results.

To make up for these shortcomings, the sun in these latitudes is very good for giving accurate direction at sunrise and sunset. Your location hardly affects its bearing. When the sun is about one-half its diameter above the horizon at sea during sunrise or sunset, its bearing is almost the same all through the tropics. (The difference is never more than 2°, and often less.)

That may sound strange.

When it's midwinter at latitude 23½°N, the sun rises well south of east and sets well south of west, just as elsewhere in the Northern Hemisphere at the time of the shortest days. But that's the time of midsummer at latitude 23½°S. Here the sun also rises south of east and sets south of west, but it makes a long arc by way of North, to make the longest days of the year.

Having thought that through, you may still be surprised that sunrise (or sunset) takes place on virtually the same bearing over such a large area. It is truly vast, stretching around the globe at its widest and more than 3,200 statute miles from north to south. That's about the distance from the Tropic of Cancer to the North Slope of Alaska, well beyond the Arctic Circle.

Directions from the Stars: Northern Hemisphere

At night by far the best guide in the Northern Hemisphere is Polaris, or the polestar or North Star. It gives North so accurately that you can use it to find the declination for your location. The traveler without compass does not need to pay attention to all the fine points of magnetic direction discussed in Chapter 8.

If you have forgotten how to find Polaris, Figure 12.2 illustrates one method.

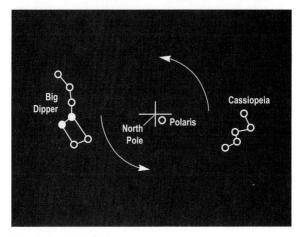

Figure 12.2 Finding Polaris.

Many people who would not call themselves experts on stars can recognize Orion with its hourglass shape, two very bright stars and three dimmer stars close together in a straight line (the belt of the mythical hunter Orion).

The belt of Orion is almost exactly on the celestial equator and so rises everywhere due East and sets due West.

So you won't forget whether it's the first star to rise and set or the last, use the middle star. You'll be within one degree or so of true direction.

Again, as with the sun, you have several minutes at rising or setting in which the bearing hardly changes.

This is a simple emergency method with only one drawback. On some nights in summer Orion rises when it's already daylight and sets before it gets dark.

Directions from the Stars: Southern Hemisphere

Polaris, that faithful night guide in northern latitudes, is invisible in the Southern Hemisphere. There is no equivalent star near the pole of the southern sky. The star nearest the celestial South Pole, which would indicate South as truly as Polaris indicates North, is of fifth magnitude, close to the limits of naked-eye visibility. You can see it only when the sky is free of both moonlight and artificial light and if your eyes are totally adapted to the dark. Its official name is Sigma Octantis; it doesn't have a common name.

By coincidence, Sigma Octantis is about as far from the celestial South Pole as Polaris is from the celestial North Pole. That's roughly one degree, or half the width one of your fingers covers in the sky with your arm outstretched.

By another coincidence, there are two stars pointing about as close to Sigma Octantis as the two that point to Polaris. Here the stars are at the end of the long arm of the Southern Cross. Sigma is not quite three hands from the nearer guide, which forms the foot of the cross.

Unfortunately, when you find a star in the right location, it may still not be the right star. Unlike Polaris, which stands away from all equally bright neighbors, Sigma has a few equally dim siblings in the constellation Octans.

For the wayfarer without compass, that makes it a pretty poor guide star. But you already have a clue for finding approximate South from the stars in the constellation Crux, the Southern Cross.

Most people who see it for the first time are disappointed. It's not nearly as large as they had expected; it isn't quite square; and the stars are not all of the same brightness. Three of them are first-magnitude stars or almost so, but one at the end of the crosspiece is a third-magnitude star, dimmer than Polaris.

Sometimes novices conjure up another group of four stars and mistake it for the Southern Cross. Don't worry about that false cross. The true Southern Cross has two closely spaced, very bright stars (Alpha and Beta Centauri) nearby for positive identification. The crosspiece roughly points to these stars, which are on the side of the brighter end star.

Now you have the Southern Cross nailed down. Its long axis points (almost) to the celestial South Pole, 27° (a skimpy three hands) away in the direction of the foot of the cross.

The point you'll get by drawing this straight line continuing the long axis of the cross misses being due South of you by about 3°. That's much better than no direction at all.

The Southern Cross does not remain visible all night and every night until you reach a latitude of about 37°S. But even near the Tropic of Capricorn it will guide you about three-quarters of the time.

The big surprise for most northerners is that you don't have to cross the equator to see this famous constellation. It's clearly visible, though low on the horizon, from Key West in the evening in April and May. If you use the method of measuring the scant three hands in the direction of the long axis Key West, you'll end up at a point in the water. But that point will be amazingly close to being south of you.

That means, of course, that you can also use this method in the tropics when the Southern Cross is in the sky.

Orion will be upside down all through the Southern Hemisphere, but quite recognizable. It will give you a reliable East when the belt stars rise, West when they set.

Directions from the Stars: Tropics

In the northernmost tropics, Polaris will guide you just as it does in higher latitudes, but the Big Dipper and Cassiopeia—always close to the horizon—disappear for long stretches.

Since Polaris is so close to the celestial North Pole, one would expect it to be visible to latitude 0°. But, as mentioned earlier, celestial objects get dimmer near the horizon. About 5° above the horizon, Polaris appears as a fourth-magnitude star, which means that even with low humidity you'd only see it in the dark of the moon. As a rule, you won't see Polaris until you are north of the latitude of the Panama Canal (9°N).

The stars in the belt of Orion are almost on the celestial equator. So all through the tropics they pass high above you. At rising and setting these three stars show East and West, as elsewhere.

Table 12.1 Direction of the sun at noon in the tropics

Latitude (degrees)	Latitude North, noon sun North	Latitude South, noon sun South
1	Mar. 24–Sept. 21	Sept. 26–Mar. 18
3	Mar. 29–Sept. 16	Oct. 1–Mar. 13
5	Apr. 3–Sept. 10	Oct. 6–Mar. 8
7	Apr. 8–Sept. 4	Oct. 11–Mar. 3
9	Apr. 13–Aug. 31	Oct. 17–Feb. 26
11	Apr. 19–Aug. 25	Oct. 22–Feb. 20
13	Apr. 25–Aug. 19	Oct. 28–Feb. 15
15	May 1–Aug. 12	Nov. 3–Feb. 9
17	May 8–Aug. 5	Nov. 10–Feb. 2
19	May 16–July 28	Nov. 18–Jan. 25
21	May 26–July 19	Nov. 27–Jan. 16
23	June 10–July 2	Dec. 12–Jan. 1

If you are very observant, Orion will look a bit strange to you in southern latitudes–it's upside down. Not only Orion but all constellations are upside down. So are the familiar markings on the moon. The waxing crescent moon looks waning, the waning crescent waxing. First quarter looks like last and last like first.

Planning: The Tropics

When planning for a trip to tropical regions, you should be aware of two quirks in the sun's behavior: it may not be overhead where you expect at some times of year, and it gets lighter and darker faster than normal.

The tropics are the only area on earth where the sun for part of the year is on the "wrong" side of the sky at noon. Sometimes it is north of you in the northern tropics, south of you in the southern.

Table 12.1 gives the approximate dates for which that is true. For example, at latitude 11°N between

April 19 and August 25, the sun will bear north of you at noon. At latitude 11°S between October 22 and February 20, the sun will bear south of you at noon.

On or near all the dates given in the table the sun will be directly overhead at noon.

The length of day, important for planning winter travel in higher latitudes, is of little concern in the tropics. Days here vary by only about an hour from the twelve-hour yearly mean. But twilight here is shorter than in higher latitudes—barely long enough to pitch the tent and boil water between sunset and darkness.

In the tropics, compass needles should be balanced for what Silva labels NME (the zone north of the magnetic equator), or ME (the zone of the magnetic equator, where the needle dips neither northward nor southward). Even if your compass wasn't intended for the right tropical zone, you can probably tilt it enough to make sure the needle swings freely.

Planning: South of the Tropics

Athletes are often interested in latitudes south of the tropics, where the seasons are reversed. In Australia, you can train for ocean swimming at Christmas. In Chile, you can train through our summer for the Winter Olympics, not just on glaciers and slush but on freshly fallen winter snow. Fanatical fly fishermen can commute between British Columbia and New Zealand in their year-round search for record trout.

One consequence of the switched seasons is the length of day. The longest days in the Southern Hemisphere are around Christmas, the shortest around the Fourth of July.

To help you plan winter activities, Table 12.2 gives length of day for southern latitudes. (During the warm season, October through March, the days are at least twelve hours long.)

You'll find the approximate length of day on the line of the nearest day in the column of the nearest latitude. For a margin of safety, you may want to use the next-higher latitude.

Table 12.2 Length of day in southern latitudes*

Date		Latitude				
		20°S	35°S	45°S	52°S	56°S
Mar.	18	12.1	12.2	12.3	12.4	12.4
	29	12.0	11.9	11.8	11.7	11.6
Apr.	8	11.8	11.5	11.2	11.0	10.8
	19	11.6	11.1	10.7	10.3	10.0
May	1	11.4	10.7	10.1	9.5	9.1
	16	11.2	10.3	9.5	8.7	8.1
	25	11.1	10.1	9.2	8.3	7.6
June	10	10.9	9.8	8.8	7.8	7.1
July	19	11.1	10.1	9.2	8.3	7.6
Aug.	5	11.3	10.5	9.8	9.1	8.6
	18	11.5	10.9	10.4	9.9	9.5
	30	11.7	11.3	10.9	10.6	10.4
Sept.	10	11.9	11.7	11.5	11.3	11.2
	21	12.1	12.0	12.0	12.0	12.0

*Time between sunrise and sunset is given in hours and tenths of hours; one-tenth of an hour equals six minutes.

Example: You're visiting Torres del Paine National Park in Chile. On August 5 at latitude 52°S, Table 12.2 shows 9.1 hours of daylight.

Example: You're considering a late-season climb of Aconcagua (32°S). The chart shows that you will have about 12 hours of daylight on March 18.

You'll get slightly more accurate results by interpolating values for dates and latitudes as described in Chapter 3. No calculations are needed, just rough approximations.

When the days are short compared to what you plan to achieve, don't forget to add the time before the start, and the time it takes to set up camp, when you plan the day.

As described in Chapter 6, in the Southern Hemisphere, compass needles do dip the other way. In

Australia and New Zealand, for example, they dip as much southward as they dip northward in the contiguous United States.

Needles are counterbalanced at the North end in southern latitudes to counteract this tendency. A Silva compass would be marked *MS* for magnetic South (small letters inside the red gate lines). Compasses balanced for South America and southern Africa are marked *SME* for south of the magnetic equator.

13.

Navigation Tricks

Until now, we've concentrated on the basic skills of navigation that every outdoorsperson should master. However, certain sports have their own bag of tricks that may be useful to others. And some types of terrain or weather conditions require skills that aren't normally encountered in other environments.

Cross-Country Travel

Most outdoorspeople tend to stick to trails. In some places, nobody should leave a trail, even for a few steps. The most obvious locations—though still not obvious for some—are the turns at switchbacks. A single hiker cutting between trail segments can start erosion that will grow with every heavy rainfall and will create two gullies in the trail, one above and one below the turn.

Other places where one must stick to trails include fragile regions such as subalpine meadows, tundra, and desert regions with cryptogamic soil (black, clumpy crust over sand). In all these areas, boot-scarred vegetation takes years to heal.

Few sane people will abandon a trail for a bushwhack without good reason. If you decide to go cross-country, be prepared for a serious thrash. Most of the time, the shortest distance between two points is along a trail, even if a map tells you otherwise.

Here are some rules of thumb for estimating time expended on various types of ground to cover the same distance:

Type of terrain	Time factor
Roads or good paths	1
Tall grass	2
Forest with light underbrush	3
Forest with thicker underbrush	4–6

Moist, low-level forests recover quickly from off-trail hiking. In the western United States and much of Canada, there are vast open areas where off-trail walking is fairly easy and does no permanent harm to the vegetation.

But the rule still holds: think hard before trading a trail for a bushwhack.

Orienteering

Orienteering as a competitive sport is generally a combination of jogging—uphill and downhill—and land navigation at its most demanding. Variations include ski orienteering (on cross-country racing equipment) and mountain bike orienteering.

In either an orienteering or an adventure race, getting lost, even for a moment, is a critical mistake. It's better to slow down and stay found than to rush along and be forced to backtrack after a mistake; small errors can cost time.

In the usual orienteering meet, the runners (or skiers or cyclists) are given a map on which from seven to fifteen control points are marked (see Figure 13.1). The racers must find them—by whatever route they choose—in the proper order and in the least possible time.

The actual control point is identified by a small (6-inch or 12-inch square) orange-and-white kite-shaped structure. You won't see it until you are quite close. To prove you have visited each control, you mark your card with a punch or colored pen provided there.

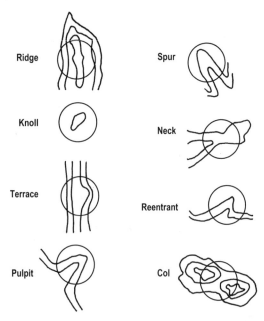

Figure 13.1 Control points commonly used in orienteering competitions, code names, and corresponding contour lines.

In most orienteering events, competitors start several minutes apart, so they can't simply follow the runner ahead but must navigate on their own.

The course setter strives to avoid "comers" at any control getting clues from "leavers." But one wonders if one clever definition of the sport, "running with cunning," refers only to the skill with map and compass. In some ways the participants in an organized meeting have it easier than individual hikers.

Racing Tips

Whether orienteering as an individual or adventure racing as a team, you are navigating cross-country to a control point marked on the map. If you happen to be at a known location (stream crossing, trail junction, building, etc.) that is at the same altitude, the best strategy may be to contour along that elevation.

Otherwise, when the choice is between approaching from above or below, it's often better to descend to the control point. This gives you the chance to see the lay of the land and decide on your next move. Furthermore you'll feel rested, rather than wiped out, when you reach the control and must make critical decisions about your next move.

Trying to "diagonal in" to a control is as likely to put you below, where ascending can be very tough, as above. It's generally better to aim a little high and then drop down as necessary. On open slopes, it may be possible to follow the compass bearing directly to the target or to triangulate your position from landmarks.

To prevent setting out in the wrong direction, determine the next bearing just before you reach a control point. Once your card is punched, you can take off without hesitation or confusion.

If you are racing in a new region, it's a good idea to relax and slow down for the first control point. This allows you to get a read on the land and provided maps. If you "dead center" the first control, you can pick up the pace to the second, and power through the rest of the course.

Though retracing steps to the last known position may be abhorrent in a race, it's often better than wandering aimlessly, looking for a control point. Once you've reoriented yourself, don't panic and frantically try to reclaim time without checking your maps. If you aren't careful, you may just compound the earlier errors and make the situation worse.

Orienteering is a popular sport in Europe whose popularity in North America is also growing rapidly. A good starting point for more information is the U.S. Orienteering Federation (www.us.orienteering.org) and the International Orienteering Federation (www .orienteering.org).

An interesting variation of orienteering is called a *rogaine* (Rugged Outdoor Group Activity Involving Navigation and Endurance). Instead of going from point to point, the runners have twenty-four hours to find all the control points in any order they wish.

Orienteering Tools

The maps used for orienteering races are redrawn so that magnetic North is at the top or lines are drawn overtop a standard true-North-up map. That eliminates the problem of allowing for declination in figuring courses and taking bearings. (So, of course, does a compass with declination adjustment, once it is set for the area.) And North-South lines, close enough for you to catch one under your compass no matter where you place it, are already drawn for you. Also, the map is on a larger scale than regular topo maps, usually 1:15,000 with 5-meter contour intervals.

The map is field-checked just before the meet. Abandoned trails are removed; so are torn-down buildings. New structures are added. Marshes that have dried up since the original topo map was made are left off, cliffs that didn't show between contour lines are drawn in, and so on. There are international specifications used for symbols on orienteering maps that provide a surprising amount of information.

For moving fast over rugged terrain, the orienteering world has developed special compasses with large needles that settle quickly; some are worn on the thumb (see Figure 13.2), while others are carried on a lanyard around the neck. These work great for on-the-fly bearings but are surprisingly expensive. An orienteering compass does not have declination adjustment, so you'll need to draw magnetic North lines on your maps if they aren't already there. Depending on the course, a standard compass may be more practical.

Because a thumb compass is meant for use on the run, the dial shows East and West reversed from normal. To go east, turn your body until the needle points to the *E* and the baseplate points the way. A thumb compass also features colors and dots to prevent confusion when exhausted; "yellow two dots" is easier to see and remember than "150°" when moving fast.

The map is normally folded so the edges point to magnetic North and is carried in the same hand, with thumb tip at your current position. For best accuracy

Figure 13.2 Brunton 6 Jet Spectra thumb compass (1.0 ounce, $90) has a super-fast settling needle for navigating on the run. Meant to be used with orienteering maps, this compass has no rotating dial or declination adjustment.

when following a bearing, take frequent sightings. With an orienteering compass, it's easy to check your direction every 30 to 60 feet while on the run; do so even more often at night.

Adventure Racing

Many adventure races do not allow the use of GPS or even altimeters—racers can be disqualified if caught using either tool. If you talk to the successful professional adventure racers, they will concede that their secret weapon is a great navigator on the team. Just as they train to improve physical conditioning, navigation skills also require constant practice; orienteering is great cross-training.

Before the start of an adventure race, organizers distribute a set of rules and maps to each team. Where orienteering events typically use 1:15,000 maps with declination lines, adventure races in the United States normally use standard USGS 1:24,000 maps. Elsewhere, particularly for big events like the Raid Gauloises, you may get as many as two dozen maps with an assortment of scales.

Teams should go over the material carefully: read *all* the race instructions, number each map in the upper left corner, and mark the appropriate map number on the instructions. On the map margins, jot down important notes such as cutoff times and key instructions. Plan on being physically, mentally, and emotionally exhausted—plus sleep deprived—while out on the course, so do what you can to make life easier.

Go through each map and exactingly plot out the UTM coordinates provided; consider adding grids or declination points to each map. Circle the checkpoints and transition areas with red or blue felt-tip pen and label them (CP1, TA2, etc.). Check the race instructions for mode of travel and to ensure that you don't use any banned trails or roads. Use an orange highlighter to mark a likely route, working backward from each control point. Also, look for alternatives so that you have a backup plan if your chosen route is impassable or too slow.

Fold the maps to show the required information for each leg. Either carry maps in a waterproof map case (and be certain it's sealed) or cover them with clear packing tape. Use an orienteering compass with a rotating capsule, such as the Brunton 1S Jet, and a UTM roamer with the appropriate scale (tape over the other scales to avoid confusion). Bring a pencil, colored pens, and a highlighter for course corrections.

It's generally best if one team member is designated navigator, though someone else may track time and pace. And everyone should stay involved by looking for landmarks and consulting maps. Pay attention to your senses: feel the humidity increase as you approach water, smell the ocean, listen for running water or traffic.

If your team gets lost, be sure to ask members independently for input on what happened and where they think they are. Sometimes the quiet person has the best instincts. When in doubt, return to your last known position.

Route Planning

Let's look over the shoulder of a runner as she decides on the course from the start to the first control point.

She'll almost certainly reject the beeline. A good course setter is not likely to arrange for such an unimaginative leg. Also, most courses are run in hill country and that eliminates most beelines; they'd go up one side of the hill and down the other. You don't gain as much time on the downhill leg as you lost in the uphill struggle. So up-and-over is longer and harder than staying level or nearly so.

Staying level means following a contour of the land, a contour line on the map, so following such a course is known as *contouring*.

Apply the backcountry travelers' law of conservation of energy: never give up elevation needlessly. The corollary is also true: every foot not climbed is a foot gained.

A time-tested formula used by orienteering runners tells us that 1 foot (or meter) of climbing uphill adds about 10 to 12.5 feet (or meters) to the horizontal distance over comparable level ground. You can substitute hiking with a load for running. Obviously that formula can apply only to moderate grades, not vertical walls.

The climb itself is easily estimated from the contour interval of your map. On our map the interval is 40 feet, so three contour lines equals about 1,200 to 1,500 feet of extra distance. If you can find a level detour of only 1,000 feet, you will save time and energy.

The runner planning her route to the vicinity of the first control avoids running by compass bearing alone. Instead she looks for a *handrail*.

This descriptive orienteering term means a long, mapped feature parallel to the direction of travel that serves as a navigational aid.

A road or trail is an obvious example; phone lines, railroad tracks, fences, and borders of fields and meadows can also act as handrails. So can natural features:

valleys, ridges, streams, shores of lakes, and edges of marshes.

If you have digested earlier chapters, you'll recognize all of these features as potential position lines. But *handrails* is a more vivid term.

You know how difficult it is to estimate distance in the landscape. What the runner needs is another position line to tell him when to abandon the handrail and turn left or right.

Such a position line in this sport is called a *catching* (or *collecting*) *feature*. This mapped feature, more or less across your direction of travel, has to be easy to recognize. It can be any one of the features listed for handrails, or a side stream, a crossing or merging trail, a building, and so on.

Using catching features is especially important for adventure racers navigating at night. Go along a bearing until you reach the first catching feature, and try to determine where you are along it. Then select another catching feature at a right angle to your path and onward.

In your own off-trail work, you may not always find a convenient collecting feature on the map just where you need one. But there often is an alternative—the bearing on some prominent peak, for example. Try to choose a bearing at about a right angle to the handrail you're following.

That's the *beam bearing* of coastwise navigators, who routinely change course when, say, an identified headland is abeam (meaning at right angles to the course). If your course is 30°, the headland—or, here, your peak—is abeam when it bears 120° (right) or 300° (left). This method wastes time in competitive running but that hardly matters for hikers. With a mirror-sighting compass and the peak or other target not far off, the beam method is surprisingly accurate.

It's most unlikely that the control you're looking for is visible from where the two position lines—handrail and catching feature—cross. Except perhaps on a course for wayfarers (beginners), the race management is not that kind to competitors.

On courses for advanced beginners to experts, the controls are progressively harder to find. The competitor tries to find a handrail and a catching feature to get him to a clearly identifiable point near the control. From that point, the *attack point,* he proceeds by micro-navigation to the control itself.

Not only are the controls shown on the map, but each competitor has a brief description of each. Most descriptions are straightforward: trail junction, stream crossing, building, for example. A circle, its center at the exact position of the control, is drawn around it on the map. You can pinpoint the control from the offset of the circle relative to the building, trail junction, or other described features.

A few map features with descriptions peculiar to the sport are shown in Figure 13.1. At first glance, some symbols look alike. But study them closer: a pulpit juts out; at a spur, the contours jump in and out; at a reentrant, they form a fishhook shape, and so on.

When for lack of a suitable handrail, runners must fall back on compass courses, they use a technique they call *aiming off.*

Nobody can run a compass course with absolute accuracy. When you come to the catching feature but can't see the target, you don't know whether to look for it to the right or the left. If you deliberately aim off to the left, however, you know your target should be on your right.

A typical example for noncompetitive aiming off is getting back to your parked car by compass. You know the exact spot on the map where you left it. The road is your catching feature. Lay a course deliberately to one side of the direct course. Until by experiment you have found a formula that fits your style better, bear off about 10°.

That adds about 18 percent to the length of your walk. If that sounds like quite a price to pay, weigh it against the fifty-fifty chance of searching in the wrong direction and having to backtrack along the road to start the search on the other side.

The method was used by old-time mariners, and it's still practiced today. Like earlier sailing masters, the captain doesn't flip a coin to decide on which side to approach, say, a harbor entrance. There's only one winning side: upwind or upcurrent. It'd be silly to have to work back against wind or current when you can get a free push.

On skis, you'd approach your car on the uphill side, then ski down to it on the road. In competitions, the runners also aim for the high ground, which usually gives a better view of the elusive controls.

Obstacles

Getting around unexpected obstacles is often a necessity when traveling cross-country. In many parts of the world, maps are woefully outdated or inadequate, so surprises are normal. Even where maps are generally good, acts of nature (flash floods, landslides, avalanches, etc.) can make course alterations necessary.

You already know how to continue a compass course across, say, a creek too wide to jump and too deep or swift to wade. First you find a landmark—perhaps a prominent, odd-shaped tree—on the far side of the creek. You then search for a crossing and walk to your landmark on the far side. You resume your original course at the landmark.

A variation on that technique involves changing course to one side by a certain angle for a certain distance; you then change course by the same angle in the opposite direction and for the same distance. When the distance is up, you resume the original course.

You can see from Figure 13.3 that the two methods are really one. In the first version, the landmark serves to measure the distance.

In the second version, you must somehow estimate the distance. The standard procedure at sea is to time how long you spend on the first leg of the detour, and turn onto the original course when you have been on the second leg for the same length of time. On land,

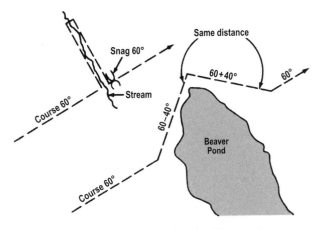

Figure 13.3 Navigating around obstacles. Top: two 90° course changes.
Bottom: two 40° course changes.

using time will only work if slope and terrain on both legs are about the same.

On land, counting steps (or paces) is another possibility. We'll talk about that presently.

The angle to turn from the base course is up to you. Two ships meeting head-on or nearly so might both turn 10°. At a creek you might turn 90°. To avoid an unmapped pond created last spring by a busy beaver, you might turn 40° (from a 60° course, first going 20°, then 100° before returning to 60°).

Here's a nautical trick that may someday be useful to you. Suppose you are walking toward a distinctive landmark, say the monument on a peak. You are not quite certain where you are, but you surely want to avoid the mapped marshy area.

Draw lines from the peak that just miss the edges of the swamp. Then measure with your compass the bearings along these lines toward the peak. Say that these bearings are 60° and 110°.

You can approach the peak from any direction and be certain to avoid the swamp as long as the peak bears less than 60° or more than 110° from you. You can see from Figure 13.4 that you'd pass south of the marsh when the bearing of the peak is less than 60°. You'd

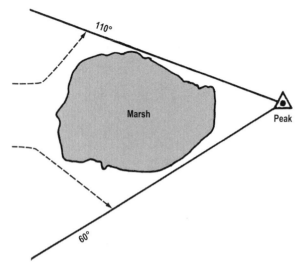

Figure 13.4 Avoiding an obstacle by using bearings and a landmark.

pass north of the swamp when the bearing is more than 110°.

Following the Route

The racers in competition want to know at all times where they are. To do that they carry a map, folded and in a plastic map case, the direction of travel facing forward, one of the runner's thumbs indicating the present position.

Carrying the map oriented to the landscape makes eminently good sense for competitors. If you have to stop and align the map with the terrain, it probably takes around fifteen seconds. If the compass is needed as well, the whole operation may take thirty seconds, breaking the rhythm of running.

Even when time is not important (what backpacker would refuse a half-minute rest?), carrying the map so it matches the landscape is a good idea. Someday it'll save you the embarrassment of having taken the left fork in the trail when clearly you should have taken the right one.

There is a time for counting paces and a time for carefree ambling. Again, we can learn from the competitive racers. They divide the course to each control into three sections, which require three different forms of navigation: rough, standard, and precision. Some call them *rough compass* (or *rough map*), *standard compass*, and so on. Others refer to a code of signal lights: green, yellow, and red.

You have navigated in a similar way in an automobile every time you tried to find a street in a strange city. At first, you rely on rough navigation on main highways or interstates to the city limits or the proper exit. Then you switch to standard navigation to find the main thoroughfare you were told to look for. And, finally, you count city blocks or traffic lights to find the side street.

Running with a handrail allows maximum speed with minimum navigation. Clearly a green-light, rough-compass section of the course.

When you are approaching the collecting feature, the yellow light goes on; you had better look for some intermediate mapped points or you'll miss the attack point. That's clearly a case of standard map-and-compass work.

From the attack point to the actual control usually means proceeding by direction and distance—a red-light, precision map-and-compass job. Here, pace counting is the only way to measure the distance.

Pace Counting

A pace means a double step. You count one each time you put your right foot down. Or your left one, if you prefer. It's an ancient method of measuring distance.

Our word *mile* comes directly from the Latin for 1,000 paces (*passus*). Enough Roman milestones have survived in place into modern times for us to know that a Roman mile was about 1,618 yards (1,479 meters). That's about 8 percent shorter than the statute mile of 1,760 yards (1,609 meters).

There's no doubt that Roman paces were measured on good and level footways. Most of us would

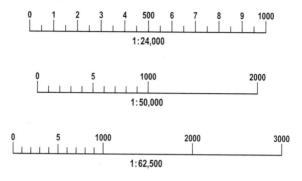

Figure 13.5 Pace gauges for even terrain.

make paces of about 5 feet (1.5 meters; distance of a military quick step) on such a track, as long as we weren't carrying appalling loads. Competitive runners under the same conditions average about 7½-foot paces (2.3 meters).

To make the task easier, you can use gauges that measure distances on the map in your pace length (see Figure 13.5). This requires different gauges for the different scales of maps used at competitions.

For hikers and other topo map users, 1:24,000 is the most likely map scale of interest. Assuming a 5-foot pace, how would you calibrate such a gauge? You'll recall that on this scale, 2,000 feet equal 1 inch. That makes 400 paces per inch, or 100 paces equal to ¼ inch. A strip of paper labeled as shown in Figure 13.5 and glued to an edge of your compass makes a simple gauge.

You could use the same gauge with negligible error with 1:25,000 maps. For a pace 1.5 meters long on such a map, the 100-pace marks would be exactly 6 millimeters apart.

That's your clue for the 1:50,000 maps frequently used in Canada, the Alps, and the rest of the world. The 100-pace marks should be exactly 3 millimeters apart.

On the 1:62,500 (or 1:63,360) maps, 1 inch equals about 1,000 paces, an easy figure to remember. (The exact equivalents are 1,042 and 1,056 paces.)

You can use these gauges on paths that aren't level and smooth if you work out your personal factors. Measure on the map as usual. Say you get 400 paces. From earlier tests, you know that it takes 50 percent more steps through the woods without a trail. So you won't reach your destination until you have counted 600 paces.

The classic way of counting is with pebbles (*calculi* in Latin, which gave our language the words *calculation* and *calculus*). But who wants to lug pebbles around? A simple abacus, made with beads on a string, is lighter.

Even without miscounting by 100 paces, don't expect great accuracy from counting paces in steep or rough terrain. In the rather tamer conditions of the competitions, even experts don't expect to get less than 10 percent error.

While we're on the subject of accuracy and error, you may want to know how far off you'll be sideways when walking a compass course. You read how to translate angular error into feet or meters at the beginning of Chapter 8. But many of us often deal with percentages, so perhaps that kind of figure is easier to remember and apply.

Don't expect to do better than a 5 to 7 percent error. That means you'll likely be 50 to 70 feet (or meters) off after walking 1,000 feet (or meters). That figure is based on a generally agreed-on error of 3° to 4°. It includes errors of the compass and of the person who carries it. It applies to walking in the open, not dodging around boulders and detouring around undergrowth in the forest.

And it's only for a one-way trip. If you make a round-trip by compass (to retrieve something you lost, for example), you may miss your present position by twice that; allow for a 100- to 140-foot (or meter) error for the round trip over a 1,000-foot (or meter) distance.

Slope and footway are not the only variables that affect distance and direction estimates. How can you keep track of a slope that changes rapidly or terrain that varies every few minutes?

Here's a typical example. You approach a lake on a well-trodden path. To reach the upper end of the lake you hop from one tuft of sour grass to the next for a while. Then, where a creek runs into the lake, you run into a stretch of sucking mud, followed by a rock slide. Next, you must climb steeply to get around a cliff that drops sheer into the lake. On the top of the cliff, fallen trees slow you down. What factors do you apply to these pace counts?

To make life easier and pace counts more realistic, competitors use a simple trick. They look for mapped checkpoints along the route and start a new pace count at each. Passing the abandoned mine, or crossing the mapped creek, you know where you are much more accurately than a pace count could tell you. You'll soon find out where it pays to count paces—say, for finding a spring—and where counting steps isn't worth the bother.

Finding the Route

Consciously looking for checkpoints has a built-in bonus for noncompetitive hikers. It helps you find the way back. You may have no intention whatsoever of returning the way you came, but sometimes the mountain gods laugh at your plans. A weather change, a minor injury, or a swollen stream may force you to return the way you came. New navigators make a startling discovery at this point: the way back looks completely strange.

Occasionally the very opposite happens. One member of your party is willing to swear that this is the snag where he tied his shoelace on the way in, there is the rock on which he rested his pack, and so on. A case of perfect recall for things never seen before.

The checkpoints you used on the way in may still stick in your memory on the way out. Stop from time to time and look back. It adds to your enjoyment, and if you have to return by the same route, the scenery will not look strange.

Carrying the images of the return trail and checkpoints in your mind will alert you when you are somewhere you aren't supposed to be.

It's not as difficult as it might seem to lose the trail. Sometimes it happens because a level side trail branches off just where the main trail changes slope abruptly. Or for some reason the main trail grows faint just where a side trail takes off. Others who have been misled may have enlarged the false trail. No wonder: they walked the false trail coming and going but walked the correct trail only once.

Orienteering maps show areas that are out of bounds for the competitors. Others must use common sense. Don't trespass on private land. Don't walk across cultivated areas. In some parts of the world that includes meadows.

In other areas, you're quite welcome to walk through fenced land as long as you leave the gates the way you found them. Of course, you would close a gate you had found closed. But some strangers think they do the rancher a favor by closing a gate someone has left open. Don't do it. You may cut off grazing cattle from their water supply, or keep well-trained horses from coming home.

One last suggestion: try to memorize the general lay of the land through which you're traveling. Often there's only one map for an entire group. Many maps have dropped out of pockets, been left far behind, or sailed away in the wind.

Just knowing in which direction the road to civilization may roughly lie could be a help.

You may have heard the advice, "Follow the drainage when lost." The idea is that water runs downhill, ending up in bigger and bigger streams, near which people are likely to live.

The logic is sound and, despite occasional lakes and waterfalls encountered, may get you out of the bush better than by merely guessing. But having an overall mental map is a great help. Otherwise, in the Canadian Rockies, for example, you might follow a drainage that leads to the Beaufort Sea.

Getting Un-Lost

More than likely, you'll be zooming along at some point and suddenly realize you are no longer "in contact with the map," a polite term for being lost. Immediately stop.

The usual advice is to retrace your steps. But that's sometimes not easy to do.

First try to reorient yourself on the map with visual clues, such as a hill or stream.

Then make a quick dead-reckoning calculation. Say it took five minutes before you realized you were no longer on the trail. How far can you be from the trail? At 2 miles (3 kilometers) per hour, you can't be more than 300 yards (250 meters) away.

Did you walk uphill, level, or downhill in the last few minutes? Did you walk into the sun, with the sun at your back, or to the left or right? Was the wind ahead, behind, or on your left or right? If you can recall any of that, you narrow the search area enormously.

When you go scouting for the lost trail, don't leave your backpack behind. You risk finding the trail but losing the pack.

The effort of finding a trail lost 300 yards back will almost everywhere pale in comparison to that required to bushwhack to an unseen destination—or even to one that's visible.

Some trails end abruptly. Game trails, for example. If you carried a rack of antlers on your head, wouldn't you follow a path in the trees that's clear of obstructions? That avoids headaches. But when you come to the edge of the meadow, you'd graze here and there, leaving no permanent spoor. Often, trails seem to end abruptly where soft ground changes to rock.

Break out your binoculars and look first in the direction you have been walking and somewhat left and right of that. Perhaps you'll spot a pyramid of stones—a cairn—to show where the trail continues.

If its builder followed tradition (pretty rare), there should be a long stone parallel to the trail on top.

If you are not sure what you see is such a marker, or if you start out hunting for one, make sure you can find the spot where the trail ended if you must retrace your steps. Walk a compass course rather than making a grazing-cow search.

Near-Shore Navigation

When you're sea kayaking and lake canoeing, some nautical navigation tools and tricks come in handy. As described in Chapter 2, nautical charts provide information on tides, currents, markers, and obstacles.

Beginning sea kayakers and canoeists will often find that 8 miles per day is a sufficient challenge. With a bit more experience, 12 to 15 miles each day is reasonable and 20 miles is quite doable with a current. Very strong paddlers can cover 40 miles a day, and even 80 miles isn't unheard of with the right conditions. These sorts of distances mean you need nautical charts or small-scale maps that have sufficient coverage.

If you are using charts, bring a set of parallel rulers (two clear plastic straight edges connected by pivoting linkage bars). These allow you to easily determine a course between two points on a map and to walk the ruler to a compass rose for an accurate bearing.

Another useful marine item is a deck-mounted compass (some bolt to the deck; others attach with straps) with a large dome for easy viewing; fancy models even have a battery-powered light. These are more convenient than a handheld compass since you can easily follow a course without setting the paddle down.

Given the effects of wind and current, you will typically achieve an accuracy of about 10° and reach a precision of 5° only with great care. The longer the distance, the more error creeps in, so it's best to keep crossings short, even if it makes for a longer trip. Rather than paddle the *rhumb line* (a direct compass course) between your starting and ending points, break the journey into shorter segments using features such as buoys, peninsulas, and islands to connect the dots.

Since wind is also a significant factor when sea kayaking, carrying a portable anemometer, used to measure the velocity of the wind, can be helpful. A headwind of less than 10 knots (smooth to choppy water) probably won't tire your arms much. But paddling into a 20-knot wind (whitecaps everywhere) is a real chore, even for experienced sea kayakers.

The average speed for sea kayaking under calm conditions (in a standard 17-foot boat, 24-inch beam, moderate payload) is about 3 knots (3.5 miles per hour; 5.6 kilometers per hour); strong paddlers in high-end kayaks can average up to 5 knots. This means you probably aren't going anywhere if you have to paddle directly into a 3-knot current (until your arms give out and you get pushed backward). Conversely, you will be zooming along at 6 knots if the current is at your stern.

Using current and tide charts (for example, http://tidesonline.com), you can more effectively plan your travel to reduce navigation errors. For example, if you must paddle straight across a 7-mile-wide channel to reach an island, the 2-hour trip will be considerably easier if you time the departure so you reach the middle of the channel at slack tide (the current will push you sideways one way the first half of the trip and the other way the second half).

More often, you will be moving diagonally across a current, so calculations become more complicated. When you're paddling near shore, it is often possible to use transits for combating drift from wind and currents. By selecting two stationary objects in line with each other (say a rock and a tree or a buoy and a point of land), you can easily determine if you are being pushed off course and compensate accordingly.

Index

*Page numbers in italics refer to tables and figures.
References to the foldout map are listed under
the Fall River Pass map heading.*

near shore navigation, 2,
    229–30. *See also* nautical
    navigation
North (magnetic/true): and
    compasses, 78–79, 91,
    102–3; and declination,
    119; movement of,
    124–25; and Polaris,
    203–5; UTM grids and, 82.
    See also declination
Northern Hemisphere, 198,
    202–3
northing, 44
North-South lines. *See* meridi-
    ans
NOS/NOAA (National Ocean
    Service/National Oceanic
    and Atmospheric
    Administration), 13, 20

obstacles, 220–22
orientation, 2, 73–74, 108–9,
    130
orienteering, 4, 132, 211–15,
    217–20
orienting lines. *See* meridians
Orion, 203, 205–6

pace counting, 223–26
paper maps, 24–29, 78–79
planimetric maps, 7–8, 58
POI (Point of Interest), 183
Polaris, 127–28, 202–5
polestar, 4, 203–4
position lines, 3, 79–81,
    113–14, 217–18
prime meridian, 45
protractor, 75–77, 83
protractor compasses. *See*
    baseplate compasses

quadrangles, 11

ranges, *50*, 51
Reed's Nautical Almanac, 22
relocating, 228–29
roamer scale, 47–48
rogaine (Rugged Outdoor
    Group Activity Involving
    Navigation and
    Endurance), 213

route: compasses and direc-
    tion, 76–81, *88*; and decli-
    nation, 130–31; finding
    the, 226–27; following,
    222–23; and GPS, 169–70,
    185, 190; pace counting,
    223–26; planning, 217–20;
    relocating, 228–29; tracks,
    169–70, 186, 190. *See also*
    map-and-compass work
ruler, 41–42, 70, 77, 104, 229
rules for declination, 133–36

safety, 1–2, 70–71, 169, 174
satellites: and ephemeris data,
    183; future of, 173; and
    GPS accuracy, 159–62; as
    GPS component, 154–58;
    history of, 152–54
scale: compasses, 84, 92, 94,
    95; distance, 31–34,
    37–40; map printing, 26;
    measuring techniques,
    40–43; nautical charts, 20;
    pace gauges, 224; repre-
    sentation, 5; series, 10,
    33–36
sea kayaking: anemometer,
    229–30; map symbols
    and, 19; marine com-
    passes, 97, 229; nautical
    charts and, 2, 20, 22; near
    shore navigation, 229–30.
    See also nautical naviga-
    tion
sections and section numbers,
    49–52
secular variation, 124
Selective Availability, 160, 172
7.5-minute (7 1/2') series,
    9–12, 22
shadows and direction,
    195–96, 200–201
Sigma Octantis (star), 204
size. *See* scale
sky (directions from the):
    equal altitude method,
    200–201; importance of,
    193–94; inaccurate meth-
    ods for, 194–96; stars, 111,
    127–28, 202–6; in the

About the Authors

W. S. Kals was a planetarium director and the author of *Practical Navigation* and *The Stargazer's Bible*, among other books. **Clyde Soles** has written four books for The Mountaineers and regularly contributes articles on outdoor equipment, nutrition, and fitness to publications such as *Backpacker*, *Outside*, *Hooked on the Outdoors*, and the online outdoor and fitness resource *GearTrends*. He also founded *Trail Runner* magazine and has been a senior editor at the climbing magazine *Rock & Ice*.

Topographic Map Symbols

—†—†—	Bridge
○ ○~	Water well, spring
	Perennial streams
	Intermittent streams
	Rapids
	Falls
	Marsh (swamp)
	Submerged marsh
	Glacier
	Intermittent lake
	Dry lake bed
	Index contour
	Intermediate contour
	Depression contours
	Road cut, fill
	Woodland
	Scrub
	Wooded marsh
	Urban area